# Encore

# Encore

✦

## Internet Learning Models That Enhance the Instrumental Music Curriculum

*Joseph V. Palazzola*

iUniverse, Inc.

New York Lincoln Shanghai

# Encore
## Internet Learning Models That Enhance the Instrumental Music Curriculum

iUniverse books may be ordered through booksellers or by contacting:

iUniverse
2021 Pine Lake Road, Suite 100
Lincoln, NE 68512
www.iuniverse.com
1-800-Authors (1-800-288-4677)

Because of the dynamic nature of the Internet, any Web addresses or links contained in this book may have changed since publication and may no longer be valid.

The views expressed in this work are solely those of the author and do not necessarily reflect the views of the publisher, and the publisher hereby disclaims any responsibility for them.

ISBN: 978-0-595-49314-2 (pbk)
ISBN: 978-0-595-61053-2 (ebk)

Printed in the United States of America

*In memory of Marian F. Palazzola, my late wife for her love, and support, in me and our son Chris.*

# Contents

# *Synopsis*

The 21$^{St}$. century is known as the information age. The technology has created tools that have changed our society forever. It has created a world that is flat again. It was common belief that during the 15$^{th}$ century; the world was flat. This was proven to be not true with the exploration of Christopher Columbus. For centuries many societies ruled other over other societies because of the superior military and technical prowess they possessed. With invention of many new scientific technologies, the internet and communication advances, many countries that were economically, militarily and natural resource challenged are now able to be a part of the information, technological explosion. They are competitive and in many areas are more able to do many jobs cheaper and more efficiently than the world powers. Therefore; the information and technological age has created a better world for all and the playing field is much more level which results in the idea that the world is flat.

What has distinguished Americans from the rest of world is our freedom to be innovative. We have always been able to create environments that produce individuals that are risk takers, visionaries and dreamers. Since we are now seeing that the world is flatter, Americans have continually been innovators. If we stop being innovative, we will fall behind those countries that were considered to be third world and catching us do to the technological advances they are able use effectively. We as Americans must continue to advance and move higher achievements. Then the world will progress with our new advancements and the whole process starts over and so on.

American education must be in the lead in regards to keeping this country in the forefront of innovation and progress. It just makes sense that if we want to remain as the leaders of the world a great effort must be given toward making sure we give our people the tools to succeed. I envision that today's educators have two areas to work on that will ensure that our young people will have the tools to compete. Therefore; all disciplines across the curriculum ought to have these two components as important ingredients to make certain significant success are achieved.

I will label each area as a holistic learning component. Each of these two (HLC) can be addressed by using the four learning models, multiple educational strategies, pedagogical, motivational and presentation techniques. These skills, strategies, models and techniques are the tools to accomplish the two holistic learning components that will produce the outcomes in our students that make them the best they can individually be and continue to raise our national standards and innovative creativeness that makes our people the world leaders in all areas.

The first holistic learning component (HLC) is "learn how to learn," (LHTL). All of our energy in the educational process must direct itself toward teaching students how to learn. In my view, the teacher's first responsibility is to give the student as many tools, experiences and practice in order to learn as an individual. The means to accomplish this LHTL will very from grade level, course or discipline. But the end result is universal. Everything leads to LHTL. The means may be different, but the ends are toward one goal. "Learn how to learn."

The second holistic learning component (HLC) is connected to the "learn how to learn" (LHTL). If a learner is able to "learn how to learn," they have "independent power" (IP). Upon further investigation into these two components and how they are connected, one can say you can't have one without the other. In order for one to be able to "learn how to learn," there must be a utilization of all of the knowledge, information, understanding, learning strategies, technological strategies and multiple literacy skills one has available in the learners tool chest in order to solve complex problem or to reach understanding.

Perhaps another way to describe the inter-relationship between the two learning components is to offer the following football metaphor:

The "learn how to learn" is the play (which results in a score) as "independent power" is the pass or run (which is the technique needed.)

Independent power is an on going process. It never stops. Individual learners are constantly discovering new ways to increase the number of learning tools to add to their tool chest. The more one has, the more power.

One of the teacher's prime responsibilities is to provide as many opportunities for students to be aware of as many strategies. This will enable the student to increase their individual power.

One of the important purposes of this book is to bring to the attention of the instrumental music teacher IP tools to be used with the internet. Instrumental music teachers not only must continue to provide leadership in teaching students performance skills and interpretation of the written score, but assist in the total educational process of the individual student. In fact, all teachers and the disciplines and courses they teach, must provide experiences throughout the curriculum that will ensure that all students "learn how to learn" and obtain as much "individual power" as possible.

Throughout my public school instrumental music tenure, I was manly concerned with teaching students how to play their instrument and performing in an ensemble. My goal was to impart as much musical information and skills as I could in order for the students to be both performers and consumers of music. As time went on, I transferred my drive of my educational delivery beyond instrumental music skills and literacy's toward the demonstration of connections of all of the arts to each other. At this point in my teaching career, I began to mature in my professional calling and educational philosophy. I discovered that it was my responsibility to teach my students about all of the arts so I began to point out to my students the commonality of the performing and visual arts. At this point, I felt like I was engaged is a very noble cause. I was not just teaching my students about music, but also how all the other arts have many characteristics in common. My thought was that I was introducing my students to all of the arts and how they fit within all civilization and culture. To me, this was validating my teaching to an even higher rank.

As I continued my teaching career, I discovered there was even more to teaching. A second revelation came to mind. I have taken my educational philosophy to another level. My educational philosophy throughout my forty years progressed from band director to arts educator to a provider of life-long learning tools. Each phase of professional development shows a progression toward more practical and personal aids for the student to have a happy and productive life. I consider myself very fortunate to metamorphose to this realization. One could be stuck with the mindset that the only important thing is to produce a player who helps the band receive a I rating at festival. I can remember those days. Thankfully, I have learned that there is more to education than teaching a student the difference between the notes a, c and a, d. The more I worked with young people; I have found they thirst for more than just to know the difference between c and d. As human beings, we are programmed to go further and develop as total beings. It goes beyond the discipline we are studying. Humans want to be the best they can be and are very imaginative and curious. Teachers have to recognize this and not be so offended when students are not as passionate as we are about our subject. They are interested to a point, but they are also driven toward that personal satisfaction of themselves and their total well being.

This book is addressing an area of the educational landscape that is exploding in all phases of the design of curriculums of today. That is the internet. The internet has made a tremendous impact on how and what we teach in the classroom in the last decade. Many classrooms across the country have the computer, technology and the internet as the focal point of many learning activities. The internet in particular has elevated the student's individual independence and power. The various teaching models and research tools that are used in conjunction with the internet has substantially enhanced learning and the gathering of information at lighting fast speed and voluminous collections of informational material. In addition to these facts, it is safe to say that the world of work has changed at an even faster and larger degree of use. Since this is the state of the world today, educators have a real responsibility and mission to make sure that students be prepared to function in this global environment. Educators must make sure that all students are equipped to have the necessary tools to be contributors in this information age global society.

Technology and the internet are not to be considered as the ends to today's educational pursuits. No, they are only the means or tools that we are now able to use to accomplish real learning and understanding that will aid in the two HLC's. They give our students the power to "learn how to learn" and independent power.

Educators must give students the opportunity to practice and experience the "new tools" of technology and the internet.

Instrumental music teachers have a wonderful opportunity to give students experiences that not only further music education, but also broaden learning of the total edification of the student. I cannot over state the importance of all teachers use the technology and internet to not only advance their own courses and disciplines, but they must also create opportunities of using these tools to give the student real life-long tools to function in today's global economy. This brings back to my original belief that since the world is flat again Americans must labor toward keeping our place as the leaders or innovators in this ever changing world economy. Carrying this belief further, our total educational commitment and push must be en route toward giving our children the tools and strategies that will ensure that they are able to "learn how to learn."

In this spirit, my focus in this book is to introduce models that will enhance student learning so that instrumental music teachers can contribute to educational commitment that I cited earlier. These models have been created to give students the experiences they need to have a superb background in using the internet. In addition, these models will produce learning activities that are meaningful and build the independent power necessary to produce students that are capable to "learn how to learn."

# 1

# *Internet Learning Models*

My supporting effort in regards to helping the instrumental music teacher integrate these internet models into the classroom is to suggest sites that coincide with the respective models. Hopefully, this will make it more convenient and doable within the classroom and the teacher's lesson schedule. After all, the instrumental teacher has many curriculum concerns to address and to add another to the mix can be overwhelming. Therefore; in order to make the belief that educators must be concerned with the introduction of more tools beyond the curriculum concerns of the course or discipline, this book should be an aid to make it easier to accomplish these ends of "learn how to learn" and "independent power." Let us not forget these models and uses of the technology will support deeply the instrumental music curriculum. Make no mistake about it; the instrumental music student will be a better well-rounded musician, arts consumer and general learner by having experiences with the internet models and other technical tools.

## Some Theoretical Considerations

The internet is a very powerful tool that is at the pinnacle of the information age. It has the capacity to give limitless amounts of information. Sometimes this information is valid and sometimes it is not. Students and any other user of the internet are now given vast amounts of information that can be extracted from hundreds of databases and websites by the click of a mouse. The new information assists the internet user with many opportunities to make personal decisions. This new feature is the fact that there is no longer the middleman in the blend. This empowers the internet user with independent power that has never before been possible. Educator's main responsibility is to give students the tools to search the internet in an efficient and correct way to extract the information properly. Perhaps the most important task of the teacher is to also give the student the ways that validates the truth of the information being considered.

"With greater access to an abundance of information, teachers and students alike need to be equipped with the skills, attitudes and thinking processes that will prepare them to be critical and responsible consumers of information" (Todd, 1999)*. This fact makes it very important to develop reasoning strategies, problem solving skills and higher level thinking. This new literacy will create students who are well informed and capable in making better decisions.

The use of the internet in the classroom has had superb results across the nation in raising standards in the ability to:

- "Capable information technology users

- Information seekers, analyzers, and evaluators

- Problem solvers and decision makers

- Communicators, collaborators, publishers, and producers

- Informed, citizens." (Jordan, 13)

That list is unquestionably impressive in regards to given students the skills, information and tools to be able to achieve the primary focus of this book which is to help the student "learn how to learn." The "independent power" is raised through these skills which are essential to accomplishing LHTL.

Information Literacy

"While increased access to resources provides information power, it also necessitates information literacy-the ability to be critical consumers of information. Information literacy has three major components" (McKenzie, 1998)*:

Prospecting:
This is the process of looking for information that is relevant and valid. The student must work on skills that will help them to find this information in an efficient and effectual manner. These skills are:

- Planning and questioning prior to searching and then as one finds the information continually cleansing and adding additional questions to refine the search to an even higher level.

- Finding search strategies that will help in procuring the information needed.

- Continues work toward finding the most pertinent and valid information-this is accomplished by analyzing and evaluating the material.

<u>Interpreting:</u>
Once the correct information is found during the search process, the knowledge and understanding must be interpreted. The following two measures must take place:

- Take the raw information and change it into information and knowledge

- The next move is to transfer, infer, and finally relate findings to the particular subject or question at hand

As you can see, there are a lot of first-rate activities that are being done. These activities are escalating the number of meaningful skills that will give an even higher number of tools to boost the "independent power" of the student.

<u>Creating New Ideas:</u>
After the material is analyzed and evaluated, the information is then synthesized and changed into new ideas and knowledge. In order for one to accomplish this task, the following is necessary:

- Inquire, exploration, problem solving and decision making

- Finding and creation of information literacy should be built within several mediums and they are:

- Visual literacy (imagery)

- Numerical literacy (number)

- Textual literacy (the written word)

One who has informational literacy skills will use the correct source of information at the right time, and will choose from various resources such as books, periodicals and the Internet.

## Learning Spaces on the Worldwide Web

In my first book, Bravo! published by iUniverse 2006, I devote a whole chapter to the four learning spaces. In order for real learning to take place, all of four of the spaces must be present in a lesson. A good balance of time must be devoted to each space for learning to be proficient. If one of these spaces is absent or a very small amount of time devoted to the learning situation, learning will not take place. The four learning spaces are: the campfire which is the informational space; the watering hole which is the conversational space; the cave which is the conceptual space and life which is the contextual space. David D. Thornburg, Ph.D., wrote an excellent book *Campfires in Cyberspace*, 1996, in this book he discusses the subject in great detail. He says that these four learning spaces are learning environments that are essential for positive learning outcomes. One of his major points he makes in *Campfires ...* is that the worldwide web and other Internet-based tools can be used to support instruction that utilizes all four of the learning spaces.

## Internet Models

Several models have been developed to support learning for students to use with the internet. These models aid the student in acquiring information and providing meaningful learning activities that enhance the curriculum and the students learning skills. In keeping with the major premise of this writing, these skills will help the student "learn how to learn." In addition, these models will give the student opportunities to practice many navigating strategies and literacy skills that are needed to be successful in using the internet as an informational gathering tool. These activities will that are used in the models are essential in accomplishing the various tasks that are required to finish the models to completion. These skills and activities required for each of the internet models are numerous and wide-ranging. Therefore; by having the chance to use the internet and the internet models, the student will increase his/her "individual power" which is essential in today's ever changing global experiences.

(A brief discussion of each of the four internet model follows. Chapters three, four, five and six, will be devoted to each model cited below in detail. In addition, examples of websites and projects will be summarized and reviewed.)

There are four internet models that will be discussed.

1.  Internet Workshop

2.   Internet Project

3.   Webquest

4.   Internet Inquiry

Internet Workshop
The goal of this model is to give students the skills needed to navigate on the internet, promote critical literacy skills and background knowledge. The student completes a simple research activity that is based on prescribed websites. These websites are chosen by the teacher. After completion of the research, students will share and exchange the information they garnered on the internet. The end result of the use of this model is that the student acquires information and then thinks critically about the information they personally found. In addition, they review and study the information the other participants in the workshop found.

Internet Project
The second model promotes a culture of learning. It also enhances interactivity and connections with other students. The Internet Project's main focus is to involve students collaboratively. One of the important skills this model develops is communication. Students use internet such as: email; online database; bulletin boards; real-time text chat (instant messages) and audio video-conferencing. These internet tools give the student capabilities beyond the regular classroom environment. The Internet Projects allows the students to experience a global occurrence.

Webquest
The third internet instructional model was developed by Bernie Dodge and Tom March. "A webquest is an inquiry-oriented activity in which some or all of the information that learners interact with comes form the resources on the internet." (Dodge and March, 1995)*. They continue by citing that Webquests reflect a variety of aspects of Marzano's (1992) Dimensions of Thinking Model. In summary, they sustained that after a student completes the activities of the webquest, they encounter many positive learning skills. The student analyzes a body of knowledge deeply. Then transforms that information in a way that demonstrates their understanding of the material and finally, they create a finished product that can be responded by others online and offline.
*Retrieved from MAT 616 Study Guide

Internet Inquiry
Problem solving and critical thinking are two very important educational standards to address. These are the major goals that only meaningful educational activity should promote. The internet certainly will support these two standards and the Internet Inquiry is a research model that will assist the student toward these ends. "The model should be focused on an essential question of inquiry, employ a variety of skills and strategies, and help students to gather and analyze the web sites they access as well as to report findings in an authentic manner." (McKenzie, 1998a; Todd, 1999)*.
This model gives the student a wonderful opportunity to research the internet. The model guides them through the five phases of a research cycle. These cycles are: question, search, analyze, compose and share.

Using the Internet Reaches Many
In addition to the many navigational strategies and literacy skills, the internet is a medium that connects people. There are no boundaries or borders. It permits instantaneous communication through the use of email and instant messaging. Therefore; it can be an activity that puts the student in contact with anyone and that includes globalization interaction with students, experts and others across the planet. This is a breathtaking opportunity for students to interact and share information never before possible with traditional modes of communication. This leads to multicultural understanding and awareness.

The internet also creates an environment that is equitable. The classroom becomes equal for all irregardless of economic, social, racial, linguistic and disabilities. The internet enables teachers to provide all kinds of learning resources. It acclimatizes opportunities for students to explore informational resources that agree with the individuals learning styles and needs.

New Literacy's
New literacy's are developed for one to be successful in using the internet. The literacy's that are used with the technology are necessary and have changed the definition of literate. New skills, insight and strategies are essential for one to be successful in exploring and gathering information on the internet. Because it is so easy to post new information, findings, results of research and materials, the internet is for-ever changing. The result is that the internet and technology is rapidly changing and the "information superhighway" is constantly moving and never stagnant. Users of the internet will have continually evaluated, synthesize

and analyze information with the new literacy's and fine new avenues to validate and verify the information gathered. In closing, these new strategies, skills and other techniques used add not only to the student' literacy, but also contribute to an increase in the number of tools for learning. The culminating result is the elevation of the student's "independent power" which equals a greater opportunity "to learn how to learn." I offer an equation which is the essence of the purpose of this writing:

Independent power plus "learn how to learn" equals the opportunity to be innovative and creative (OTBIC)

Or

IP + LHTL = OTBIC

# 2

## _Internet Workshop_

The Internet Workshop is used to accomplish five areas:

- Introduce a new unit

- Build background knowledge and information

- Increase specific content information

- Awareness and practice of various navigational strategies that will aid in finding information on the internet

- Concentrate on critical literacy's that are necessary when using the internet

The Internet Workshop will also extend:

- Content knowledge

- Strategies for using network information resources

- Skills that support collaboration by providing avenues for students to exchange and share information

Procedure for the Internet Workshop:
There are four steps the teacher will follow to prepare the Internet Workshop for the students:

1.  Locate several sites that contain appropriate information that is related to the course content. Bookmark those sites for future work.

2.  Create the student activities for the students. Provide open-ended questions for the students that will guide them in the project. (Unless your goal is to develop critical literacy skills.)

3. Give the students a time frame for the students to follow in completing the project.

4. Culminate the project with the students sharing and exchanging information.

Authors Note to the Reader:
My experience throughout my years in the public schools was that there is never enough time to get all of the things done that has to be accomplished during the school day. I also found that I had so many after school rehearsals and planning sessions that it was just physically impossible to add to the work load. My intention is to help by providing some sites that I have discovered on the internet to aid you. Thus cutting out a few steps that you do not have to worry about and since I now have the time to do so, I will provide you with some suggested sites to use in your classroom. I will list a few sites for not only the Internet Workshop which is the subject of this chapter, but I will also provide additional sites and projects for the other models. My goal is to make it as easy for you as possible. Perhaps later you can do some investigating of internet projects on your own when the time is right for you. If not, I am providing good samples in my view for you to look at as possible projects for your students. The one very important fact that must be made is that the internet is every changing and sometimes sites and projects are either outdated or even removed from the internet for one reason or another. So keep in mind that the internet is every changing on a daily basis. Another tip I can give you is if you find a project on the internet that ask for payment or a membership fee, I would suggest you not get involved with it. First of all, there are many fine sites and projects posted on the internet that are free and also keep in mind of your budget concerns.

The Internet Workshop-Tailor made for your classroom.
I have done many searches to find appropriate Internet Workshops. There are some available, but not many. The reason for this in my opinion is that Internet Workshops are very personal projects designed for the individual classroom. Many teachers invent their own workshop that are designed and created for the teachers own classroom. Since the Internet Workshops main focus is to build new information, many teachers use one workshop to spur other Internet Workshops that add more and more new information to the individual classrooms overall quests. Each workshop is related to the previous one and so on. This fact reminds me of the Concept Attainment Strategy of the Understanding Learning Model. "One indicator of student success is the number of concepts that the stu-

dent understands. The Concept Attainment Strategy allows a student to build concepts and understanding relationships between the different concepts." (Palazzola, 37). In other words, instead of concepts, the student is able to build new information sources by the study of several related workshops.

I have found a number of wonderful sites that are well worth your time to study in detail. It is a must for those that are interested in developing an Internet Workshop. This site is loaded with many articles, suggestions and search directories that will help any teacher with creating well organized and meaningful projects that will be positive experiences and learning activities that will certainly provide opportunities for students to develop and nurture IP and LHTL.

I will furnish the title of the workshop, the name of the author and date published, and the websites address. In addition, I will also provide a brief explanation of the features of the site, ease of finding information, the amounts of information available and the comments in regards to the sites relevancy and timeliness. Finally I offer my opinion or recommendation of the project. The actual criteria subheadings and the order used for the review are noted below. (Some of these sites do have information and suggestions to use for the instrumental music classroom).

In-Dept Review of an Internet Website
(It is suggested, in order to adequately gain real understanding of the website reviews reported in this book, the user-teacher or student-log onto the site as you read the assessment. This will ensure a clearer awareness and picture of what the reviewer is relaying to the user. It helps to have the site in front of you and one can experience the various features and options available within the site. We certainly learn with more efficiency when we are doing hands-on activities.)

Review Criteria:

- Title
- Web Address
- Author
- Publication Date

- Features

- Ease of Finding Information

- Current/Relevancy

- Amount of Information

- Recommendation

Title:
*Internet Workshop: Making Time for Literacy*
This is a premier source for teachers to use in designing and creating Internet Workshops. A must read before a teacher begins to design and creation of an Internet Workshop.

Website address:

http://www.readingonline.org/electronic/RT/2-02_column/

Author:
Donald J. Leu, Jr. PH.D., Professor at Syracuse University.

Publication Date: February 2002

Features:
The website gives the teacher many outstanding examples of literacy's that can be incorporated into the workshop activities. There are links and other appropriate sites as resources that can be utilized in regards to teaching thru the internet.
In addition, four excellent search engines are suggested. These search engines are wonderful sources for teachers to find appropriate sites that will make the internet experience user friendly and child prove.
The four search engines are:

- Yahooligans

- Ask Jeeves for kids

- Searchopolis

- Kids Click

These search engines are essentially directories and databases of kid friendly sites that will allow the teacher to save search and verification time because the sources listed are appropriate and safe for children of all ages. This is a great benefit to the teacher because it will make the searches of sites more efficient. It will make your job in creating the Internet Workshop easier and less stressful in regards to putting together a meaningful and sound project.

Ease of Finding Information:
The site describes in detail the four steps of preparation that the teacher prescribes to in developing an Internet Workshop.

- Strategy-the location of sites. Each site must be:

  - Bookmarked

  - Save for children of all age levels

  - Limit random surfing from the search

  - Appropriate for children

- The four search engines:

  - Yahooligans-This search engines consists of directories that are suitable for children from (7-12). The user clicks on the icon and follows the prompts.

  - Ask Jeeves-This is a directory and search engine that is based on natural language. The user types a question and the engine will provide sites to use.

  - Searchopolis-This is another directory and search engine organized for elementary, middle school and high school aged students. Like the previous engines the user types the topic in the dialogue box and appropriate sites will be suggested to the user. Another nice feature is the menu on the left side of the home page. This menu offers several indices. Just click on the indices and search for sites. Searchopolis can be a rather complicated site to use for searching. It is important to find an engine that is quick and this engine not real user friendly. The importance of this engine is it does offer many options worth looking into.

  - Kids Click-This engine is a web search for children by librarians. It has many topics available to search. Kids Click offers a very easy way to locate sites. One excellent feature of this is that it identifies the reading level of each site.

A second strategy is for the teacher to select one of several central sites. The central site contains an extensive and well organized set of links for the content areas. In addition to being a suitable, the teacher must find a site that does not change. It is consistently not going to vary and continue to be valid and accurate.

- Design an activity-The design is a five part phase.

  - The teacher first starts with an introduction of the site that the students will use to complete the project.

  - Secondly, it is important to develop important background information

  - The third phase is to develop strategies to navigate and search within the internet.

  - Next, develop critical literacy's to be meaningful and effective for internet use.

  - Finally, the teacher must provide open-ended questions that allow students to have choices about the information that they will bring back to the class and share in the final class activity. The reason for this is to encourage diverse information back for the discussion phase. It would be counter productive if all students would bring back the same information.

- The third step of the Internet Workshop process is completes the project. Set-up a schedule of activities.

- The final step is the presentation. How will the information found by each student or even group of students be brought back to the total group? The format is a workshop and information will be shared for all to discuss, question and comment on. The information must be shared and time for assessing and evaluating must be provided. Students will share their work as the conclusion of the exercise. They share their findings in a number of ways. Some of the ways are to give and compare their findings that they have discovered. This is a a wonderful and meaningful way to learn. There also is a sense of ownership because new and different information will be brought to the class for discussion and evaluation.

In closing, one of the most meaningful uses of the workshop is to use the workshop to springboard further workshops that keep building and spur additional quests that create other ways to learn and practice on the internet as a learning tool.

Current/Relevancy: This site is current and filled with outstanding up-to-date information. The search engines are constantly posting new and improved sites that will keep the educator and students contemporary.

Amount of Information: The website and the various search engines that are suggested are voluminous in information. In addition, many of the sites found in the databases are linked to even more meaningful and worthwhile information.

Recommendation:
The site has many additional sites, articles, suggestions and strategies needed to provide a meaningful experience. I must first source!!!

Below is one example of the Internet Workshops that was found using a Google search.

Title:
*Suite 101 enter curious*
This site provides general information for the teacher. Its main focus of information is to educate the teacher on the Internet Workshop.

Website address:
http://teachingtechnology.suite101.com/article.cfm/internet_workshop

Author:
Shaun Krasner is a middle school technology teacher at a charter school.
Date: September of 2006

Areas of Interest:
The site gives an explanation of the four steps of the Internet Workshop. It has many sub topic areas on the home page that gives the teacher many examples of appropriate internet workshop articles; references; reflect blogs; discussion; online courses; teacher and technological messages from the experts.

Activities:
There are no activities listed. The websites focus is to make available professional resources for the educator. It also provides avenues for the professional to create communities that will share information and a forum to interact. There is no par-

ticular project suggested, but it is well worth the interested professional's time to surf the many areas to peruse.

Recommendation:
As suggested earlier, this website is a wonderful resource that teachers can use as a place to study and get ideas in regards to creating Internet Workshops. There is a wealth of information and articles that will certainly supply the teacher with the correct tools to create a successful original Internet Workshop tailored for the individual classroom.

In concluding this chapter, it was pointed out that the reviewer was not able to find specific Internet Workshop examples. The reason being is that many of these projects are designed and produced by the teacher. It is an experience based on the curriculum and needs of the students of the individual classroom. Remember it is the teacher's job to put together the websites and resources the students are to use in completing the project. My suggestion is to study very carefully the information that is found in the two mentioned websites and devise your own. Perhaps after you have successfully created and used your Internet Workshop, you will pass it onto other instrumental teachers and this will snowball into a whole list of possible Internet Workshops for our instrumental classrooms. Remember the key to the Internet Workshop is to introduce new units or new information.

# 3

# *Internet Project*

What is the Internet Project? The Internet Project is collaborative experience. It is a model that gives students the opportunity to work with other students from other locations than their own classroom. They are given the chance to collaborate with students from other classrooms within their school, school districts, states and countries. It can be an experience that can span from a local setting to a global schoolhouse. It is very exciting to think that there is an opportunity to cooperate with each other with other students from very different cultures and diverse environments. Because they are working with others across the globe, they are able to use many technological tools such as emailing and publishing work on websites that will enable the students to improve in reading and writing. Reading and writing does improve when students have an authentic audience to communicate with.

Two Types of Internet Projects: (website project and the spontaneous project)

The first Internet Project is known as a website project. This a good point to start. These are tasks that have been already designed and are ongoing. Teachers can find these ventures by going to websites that have directories of projects that are registered. Some of these projects are open and the teacher can enter their class in the mission. Other undertakings are continuing, but they may be closed for additional classes. It is important to first go to the internet project's directory websites and study the various and check on the status of the project. It will certainly safe time in finding a suitable project.

The website project is a fine way for the teacher to truly understand the inner workings of an Internet Project. It offers the chance for the teacher and student to witness and experience the initial focus of joint activities. These website projects provide clear direct directions and instructional resources. In addition, each mission has a project coordinator to guide and answer questions. It is always good to have one available for consultation and clarification of activities and experiences.

The best advice one can give is that it is good to be able to find an ongoing open project with a coordinator to help the teacher and class to move through the experience. It gives the teacher and students the confidence to be successful in entering into a new avenue of learning and collaboration. An existing project will ensure a fine occurrence that will lay the foundation success and good experiences that can lead to the second type of Internet Project.

The second kind is the spontaneous project. These endeavors are created by the teacher. These projects are designed for the particular class and its special interests and development of literacy's that will benefit that class. After the idea of the project is cited, the class invites other classrooms to participate. By registering the project and its description, the fun begins if other classes decide to enter into the project. A snowball effect will take place and many new insights and ideas will be studied by many.

There are four steps or procedures of the spontaneous project:

1.  Step one is to plan the learning goals.

    *   Summary of the project
    *   List of objectives or goals
    *   Expectations for collaboration of partners
    *   Timeline for the project

2.  Post the projects description and timeline in a registry website. This should be done in advanced. Several months of lead time is necessary.

3.  Arrangements must be made with other teachers who chose to participate in the project. Collaborative details must be laid out and agreed to so that a smooth project can be executed.

4.  Complete the project by using the Internet Workshop Model and posting the information found in the classroom and exchange with other classes their Internet Workshop findings.

Examples of Collaboration: There are different ways or tools that the students can use to participate in the project.

- The students can email each other in regards to their topics and explorations.

- They can contribute via posting data and other pertinent information in regards to the project in a common site. This is a way that the students can compare and analyze results.

Choosing an Internet Project: (website project)

The first step in starting to investigate the Internet Project is to choose the proper project to get involved with. As suggested, it is best to start with an existing project. If the teacher wishes to carry the existing Internet Project to a more customized activity for his/her classroom, it is essential to be comfortable with an open project that can act as a model for future tailored endeavor.

The best place to embark is a review of a few popular websites that act as directories, registries and networks for the various Internet Projects available for collaboration.

Additional Internet Project Background Information: The most important bit of advice one can give is the importance of websites that are directories or registries of Internet Projects. These sites lead the teacher to appropriate Internet Projects. Since the Internet Project is a model that is a collaborative activity, it is essential for the teacher to find an enterprise that is registered and active or ongoing. That is why it is very important to explore these directories before one selects an appropriate project. It will ensure an efficient search and help in providing an appropriate endeavor for the particular area one wishes to pursue.

The Internet Project Experience:
The Internet Project is a very meaningful activity that will aid the student in developing collaboration and use of the tools of the technology. It also is instrumental in developing experiences that are at the forefront in today's workplace environment. Since we are in a global economy and solution orientated work modes in many businesses, it is very important for students to practice and experience collaborative or cooperative team building. By using Internet Projects, the teacher can provide many experiences that support this kind of environment. One can compare the Internet Project with the Interpersonal Learning Model.

The prime goal of the Interpersonal Learning Model is to develop personal relationships. Students not only learn content, but they also connect what they have experienced to the real world and make connections with each other. This is a wonderful way for students to share and build collaborative experiences.

As in chapter two, the following format will be used to review the suggested Internet Project websites:

In-Dept Review of Internet Websites

Review Criteria:

- Title

- Web Address

- Author

- Publication Date

- Features

- Ease of Finding Information

- Current/Relevancy

- Amount of Information

- Recommendation

The two websites are directories and vehicles for finding Internet Website projects. The two sites that will be explored are: *Online Collaborative Projects: Locating Projects and iEARN.*

Title:
*Online Collaborative Projects: Locating Projects*

Website addresses:
http://annettelamb.com/tap/topic1b.htm

Author: Annette Lamb

<u>Publication Date:</u> June 2000 updated April 2002.

<u>Features:</u>
The first action that is recommended to the teacher after the site is opened is to begin an exploration of the various links displayed on the opening page. A general perusing of the site is suggested. After a general browsing is completed to see what is available on the website, go back to the home page and find the link labeled *Global Schoolhouse Hihlites*. This link is the most appropriate in finding Internet Projects. *Global Schoolhouse* (Copyright 2000) is a virtual meeting place for teachers, students, parents and anyone interested in interacting, collaborating, publishing, or developing and finding learning sources. The site is a superb place to find many Internet Projects that are current and appropriate for many classroom situations. One can find projects of many topics including music that are registered and classified for the educator to easily find. The site takes the perspective participant educator to a user-friendly page that directs a search based on the disposition of the project such as if it is current, a future project, open for use, and the age level of the student. It continues further with an advanced search that narrows the search even more. When the search is completed, the site will take you to a listing of the various sites that were chosen by the user and a page of the project, a brief description, and student activities are reviewed.

Global Schoolhouse link:
http://www.globalschoolnet.org/GSH/

Below is an example : The educator is urged to take a look at it on the website.
Basic Project Information
Title: Music Around the World (ID:2970)
Begin & End Dates: 12/13/05 to 12/31/08
Number of Classrooms: any
Age Range: 5 to 21 years
Target Audience: Anyone

<u>CLICK HERE</u> to send email to project coordinator.
Project Registration URL: <u>http://cbmusic.blogspot.com/</u>

As one can see, it is a well laid out synopsis with all the pertinent information needed for one to consider as a possible Internet Project.

Another important feature of the search page is that it gives the dates that the projects were registered. This is very important in regards to making an informed decision as to the relevancy and timeliness of the project.

The browsing feature of the site is a fantastic because it allows for the educator to see many examples of what is available. It also gives the teacher ideas for possible spontaneous projects that could be designed and created.

Below is another example of an instrumental music Internet Project: Check it out on the website.
Basic Project Information
Title: The Virtual Museum of Music Inventions (ID:141)
Begin & End Dates: 9/01/99 to 6/30/10
Number of Classrooms: 100
Age Range: 9 to 13 years
Target Audience: Anyone

Ease of Finding Information: The homepage is a great starting point. The areas of information are clearly marked. The user is only has to click on the highlighted phrases and the designated area pops-up. When the new page is located, it is also clearly marked for additional links and related information.

Current/Relevancy: The site is current and abundant with excellent information. Because this site is an international directory, the most up-to-date and pertinent information is available.

Amount of Information: *Online Collaborative Projects: Locating Projects* is a staggering network. The user has wonderful opportunities to explorer many directories and even interpersonal exchanges for students. The directories list many projects that are appropriate and the user can be assured that they are valid and worthwhile educational pursuits for the classroom.

Recommendation:
*Global Schoolhouse* is a must see first site. It is in my opinion the most prolific site at this point in time. It will help the teacher with searching and finding meaningful projects. In addition, it would really be to ones advantage to first browse through the original site *Online Collaborative Projects: Locating Projects* which is a treasure of information. In addition, the website directs one to other links that endorse wonderful learning resources that utilize the internet as a powerful tool to orchestrate IP and LHTL.

The second website that is an excellent example to locate Internet Projects is *iLearn*. This website like *The Global School House* is a global network for collaborative projects.

Title: *iEARN: International Educational and Resource Network*

This is an excellent website that acts as a global network of collaborative projects. It has a wealth of listings of various projects of many topics to choose from.

Web address: http://www.iearn.org/index.html

<u>Author:</u>

This website is a group venture with no single person listed as its founder or author. Below is a statement quoted from the "about us" tab located at the top of the home page:

"iEARN (International Education and Resource Network) is a non-profit organization made up of over 20,000 schools in more than 115 countries. iEARN empowers teachers and young people to work together online using the Internet and other new communications technologies. Over 1,000,000 students each day are engaged in collaborative project work worldwide."

<u>Publication Date:</u> iEARN was developed in 1988.

<u>Features:</u>
In addition to being a very good place to educate teachers and students to internet collaborative projects, there are many related articles, workshops and resources for teachers and students to study technologies and areas of interest as it relates to the internet. One can learn quite a bit about the website by clicking on the "about us" icon located at the top of the home page. There is a very good explanation of the purpose of the website.

"iEARN is: (Below is quoted directly from the site.)

- an inclusive and culturally diverse community

- a safe and structured environment in which young people can communicate

- an opportunity to apply knowledge in service-learning projects

- a community of educators and learners making a difference as part of the educational process

These projects enable students to develop:

- research and critical thinking skills

- experience with new technologies

- cultural awareness

- the habit of getting involved in community issues"

As one can see, the website has a very inclusive and expansive mission.

iEARN is the largest non-profit in the world network designed to help teachers and students in technologies and collaborative projects

Activities:
Since the website is a network of numerous projects, articles, professional development workshops, online teacher training, interactive forums, news, and a database of projects, there are many ways to lean and participate within the website.

Ease of Finding Information: The homepage is clearly marked and the areas of use are found at the top of the page. They are easily assessed and clearly marked with icons. By simple clicking on the icon, the user will go directly to a homepage with many additional links and information to explorer.

Current/Relevancy: This site is current and up-to-date with information that is collaborated by and international membership of 20,000 schools and 115 countries.

Amount of Information: The information is staggering and international in scope. The fact that member users can communicate and interact with each other is a great feature. The sharing of ideas and lessons and how they work is current and encourages creativity and expansion of new information.

Recommendations:
*iEarn* is just a wealth of information for the classroom teacher and students. It is definitely a starting point to learn and locate projects for the classroom. It is website that can be considered a bible of collaborative projects and is a resource that is meaningful toward successful internet experiences for the student.

Additional Websites to consider:

There are many websites listed on the internet that are excellent for educators to find Internet Projects. The two that have been cited and reviewed in this chapter are truly outstanding examples of meaningful and well worth the teacher's time to check out. The good news is that these sites are ongoing and constantly improving. In some cases, sites disappear almost daily. It is important to realize this can and does happen for one reason or another. This chapter is dedicated to finding websites that are going to be in existence, but there are no guarantees. Below are a few more that are recommended highly as legitimate and likely to be around for a while. These websites are not only excellent sources to consider. They also add to the list of internet and collaborative projects that are meaningful and worthwhile to enhance the learning landscape of the classroom. One will notice that many of these projects are overlapped from one website directory or network to the next which validates the project of the duplication. Duplication of projects from one directory to the next makes that project usually indicates even more meaningful and legitimate. Note this is not always true, the teacher is the foremost authority in finding the best project for the teacher's classroom situation. Therefore; these additional websites are highly recommended because of their wealth of information and strong reputation.

*Kidlink* http://www.kidlink.org/KIDPROJ/quick.html
*Kidlink* is an excellent resource. The website is sponsored by and organization that has put together a large database of worthwhile projects that will help the teacher and student in finding appropriate places where secondary aged students up to age of 15 can have a wonderful collaborative experience with other liked aged students. *Kidlink* is international in scope and very user-friendly in navigating throughout the site. There is one music project worth studying. The project finished its work in 1998, but it is a fine example to acquire ideas for spontaneous projects.

In conclusion:
There are many directories and networks devoted to internet and collaborative project found on the internet. It is suggested that teachers and students type in the search engines such as Google, Yahoo and other popular engines the phrase "internet and or collaborative projects." When the search is complete, the user can browse through the various websites to locate the appropriate site that would be appropriate for the classroom situation and topic of the project that will aid the teaching situation. One important point to report is the fact that the internet and its multiple databases of websites is an every changing phenomenon. It is not always current since the posting of sites is very fluid. It changes daily. This unending revolving and updating is good if the new additions are all legitimate and valid. But this is not always the case. It is up to the teacher or internet user to ferret through the database of sites and verify and validate the information and content of the site. Therefore; the teacher and or student must continue to

increase their competence and "independent power" in making sure the suggested sites that are listed are appropriate, meaningful, current and valid sources of information and projects that will enhance the classroom's Internet Project experience.

# 4

## *WebQuest*

What is a Webquest?

A WebQuest is an online lesson or unit format that gives the student a precise outline and step-by step sequence of events to accomplish tasks that provide learning and new knowledge for the learner.

There are six elements that are present in WebQuest.

- WebQuests are activities that are inquiry-orientated.

- Students are engaged in tasks which are doable and interesting.

- WebQuests give students opportunities to raise their thinking skills in experiences of analysis, synthesis and evaluation.

- Students take the information found during the WebQuest process and transform the information into useful and meaningful new knowledge.

- By using pre-determined resources from the internet and other sources, students are able to focus their energy on using information rather than retrieving information.

- The WebQuest time-line can either be long or a short time in duration.

The Six Elements of the WebQuest:

- Introduction: The introduction of the WebQuest is the place where the student's interests are piqued. The introduction sets the stage and motivates the student toward an engaging activity. It provides curiosity, interest and anticipation in the student to forge ahead and accomplish the completion of the project. In addition, the introduction provides the learner background information and preview what it is to come. In summary, it promotes excitement and curiosity that energizes the student in a positive way toward learning via a lesson or unit.

- Task: The WebQuest task element is devoted to giving the student a description of what is expected of the student both in process and product. It gives the "game plan." In addition, it promotes further areas of importance.

  - The tasks supply goals and focus for the learner.

  - A well designed task is doable and engaging.

  - The task encourages thinking on a the part of the learner rather than just rote learning.

- Resources: Included in WebQuests are a number of resources. These resources are provided by the teacher and found on the internet. The teacher gives these resources to the student in order for the work of the WebQuest to be completed. As cited earlier, these resources are to be used by the students rather than located by the student. These resources are from a variety of places. They can be web documents, experts who are found online and available via the emails, instant messaging, voice messaging, chat rooms, and other searchable databases. In addition to these resources, magazines both hardcopy and online, newspapers both hardcopy and online, and DCD-ROM's are also used.

- Process: The task is completed by a step-by step process. The process must be described is a very clear, precise and doable way to ensure that the student can independently accomplish the entire task in an efficient manner. If the teacher does not provide adequate directions and explanations, the whole purpose of working and enhancing the curriculum by using the internet is defeated. In addition, the educator must provide proper and germane resources that are accessible and navigated in a timely and doable manner. The teacher must continue throughout the exercise to monitor and assist the student as needed to ensure an on task experience that benefits progress and real meaningful learning. In summation, the success of the project is to provide the learner an adequate step-by-step process and doable activity that makes the task achievable for the learner.

- Evaluation: The teacher should give students clearly defined rubrics that will assist the student to assess what was accomplished during the project. "This helps both the students and teachers understand elements of the process and product through which students are expected to demonstrate their learning." (Jordon, 35).

- Conclusion: The place where the student reflects on what was learned is perhaps the most meaningful. Information was used to find new knowledge. This new knowledge was explored, investigated, and verified. The result is that the student will be motivated to continue additional investigations on the topic or other related topics that will add to additional pursuit of finding new and exciting knowledge.

Why is the WebQuest an important project?
The Webquest give the student learner access to:

- Information that is timely and authentic.

- Tasks that is authentic.

- Problems that encourage creativity.

- Questions are raised through the investigation of additional clarification and further exploration.

There are twelve kinds of tasks that WebQuests explore:

1. Journalistic

2. Design

3. Consensus

4. Creative product

5. Retelling

6. Compilation

7. Mystery

8. Persuasion

9. Self-knowledge

10. Analytical

11. Scientific

12. Judgment

As one can see, there is a great variety in the kinds of tasks that can be used in WebQuests project. Also WebQuests are used in a wide range of curriculum areas and age levels.

Developing WebQuests: It is recommended that teachers begin studying various WebQuests that are proven and meaningful ongoing projects before developing WebQuests for their classrooms. The teacher can find some excellent examples if searches are initiated. Later in this chapter, sample WebQuests will be reviewed for future considerations. These WebQuests provide training material, templates, worksheets and other pertinent material that will help in understanding what a meaningful and successful WebQuests entails.

Developing WebQuests requires the ability to:

• Find appropriate resources for the topic that is being investigated.

• Use Web editor to create web pages for the project.

• Organize the students so they are able to work in a positive environment that leads to success.

Selecting the proper topic:

• Expand on an existing lesson.

• The topic is based on standards of the curriculum.

• An adequate number of text and websites should be available for the topic to be explored properly for the learner to have a good experience.

• The topic requires understanding and the transformation of knowledge.

The next section of this chapter will be devoted to reviewing websites. The first reviewed websites are directories or resources of WebQuest projects and the second group will be music WebQuests.

Below find the criteria used in reviewing these directories and resources:

• Title

- Web Address

- Author

- Publication Date

- Features

- Ease of Finding Information

- Current/Relevancy

- Amount of Information

- Recommendation

Directories, Resources or Databases:
Title: *WebQuests at San Diego State University*

Web Address:
http://webquest.sdsu.edu/webquest.html

Author: This website is put together by the fathers of the WebQuest Bernie Dodge and Tom March

Publication Date: The website was first initiated in 1995. The website continually up-dated and remains as on the cutting edge in regards to current WebQuest projects and information.

Features:
The main page is called The WebQuest Page. A large square fills the page. Within the square are several topics. They include: Overview and FAQ; Fan Mail; Portals; Training Materials; What's New; Examples and Search. When the user places the cursor within each phrase or topic within the square and clicks, a page is displayed with additional information and links that are related to the topic.

The user can surf through all of the topics listed on The WebQuest Page and consider all of the topics, but to give one a taste of what is available below is a sample of some of the links or sub areas of the topics.

Portals:

- News
- Forum
- Articles
- Find a WebQuest
- Submit a WebQuest
- QuestGarden: Create WebQuests

Training Materials: Included in this page are three areas and Within each area is additional links.

- Overview and Underpinnings-One of the sub-links within this section is Education World which has additional links devoted to such subjects as how to create a WebQuest and an interview with WebQuest co-founder Bernie Dodge.
- Specific Aspects-One of the links is dedicated to developing search techniques.
- Complete Workshops-One of the links in this area is Internet Expeditions: Creating WebQuest Learning Environment.

Ease in Finding Information:
This website is wonderful and very user-friendly. The graphics are pronounced and by simply pointing the cursor on the topic and clicking, the user can locate useful and helpful information. The information is current, pertinent and meaningful.

Current and Relevancy:
The user will find that the site is extremely significant in regards to using the WebQuest as a vehicle toward understanding and finding appropriate projects for the learner to participate and experience. One area within the Portals topic located on The WebQuest Page is the many opportunities for educators to connect via the internet. There is a place for professionals to make comments regarding various topics associated with the use and participation with WebQuests. If the user surfs through other areas of The WebQuest Page, one can find many

other features such as: Announcements; News; Work in Progress; Research and Evaluation; Rubrics and WebQuest ideas.

## Amount of Information:
The amount of information found within the website is staggering. It is without a doubt one of the best resources available. The potential user of the website must take a test drive through all of the topics and links to really get a good understanding of the importance of this site to the educator.

## Recommendation:
One who is seriously considering the WebQuest as an internet project model as an activity for learners to develop and build LHTL and IP, should put this website as the number one option. The site put together by the two founders of the WebQuest is the premier authoritative site to research before one initiates the WebQuest model in the classroom.

Title: *Music Education Technology*

Web Address: http://metmagazine.com/mag/wonderful_world_webquests/

Author: Steve Oppenheimer. Editor-in-Chief
        2007 Penton Media, Inc.

Publication Date: A current periodical for music educators.

## Features:
Music Education Technology is an online newsmagazine dedicated to music education and music technologies. Within the site that is listed in the website below, is an article written by Tom Rudolph who is a director of music in Haverford, Pennsylvania Schools. In addition, Mr. Rudolph is president of the Technology Institute for Music. The article is "Wonderful World of WebQuests." The educator will find that this article is extremely informative which covers the following areas:

- What is a WebQuest?

- Parts of the WebQuest

- WebQuest Support Sites (within this area there is a wonderful site that is suggested-www.bestwebquest.com

- Ready Made WebQuests

Included in these areas are additional links to other websites that is truly excellent resources and gives information that is crucial to understanding and awareness of WebQuests. As the educator explorers this article, one can see the value of this article, but also those referenced articles and websites that are suggested. In addition, the magazines is full of excellent articles in regards to many issues associated with music lessons, technology and other current trends in the music education field.

<u>Features:</u>
The newsmagazine offers many departments that one can research and study. These departments can be accessed by moving the curser and clicking then the appropriate page will appear. On the left side of the homepage the following departments are displayed:

- Music Education

  - Lesson Plans

  - Tell us about your Program

  - Conferences

  - Regional Seminars

  - TI: ME (The Technology Institute for Music Education-Improving Music Education through Technology)

- Editorial

- Related Interest

- For Advertisers

There is also links found on the homepage for one to sign-up for a free subscription to the magazine.

## Ease of Finding the Information:
All of the various features are well displayed on the homepage and easily navigated. The topics are clearly marked.

## Current or Relevancy:
This monthly newsmagazine is chocked full of applicable information that is essential for today's technological laden educational environment. In order for the music educator to keep up with current technological advances, it is extremely salient for one to have a resource to have in the educator's toolbox. Therefore; the music educator must continue to be current in order to an affective professional who makes learning meaningful and motivating to the student. Remember our main goal is to continue to make sure that the educational process for students be directed toward projects and learning activities that enhance student's LHL and IP experiences. This magazine is an important tool to have and should be used to advance the current instrumental classroom in providing information of not only internet projects, but also to introduce new areas of music education as it relates to the technology.

## Amount of Information:
This site provides ample information in regards to technology, workshops, seminars, and professional articles.

## Recommendation:
The Music Education Technology magazine is an outstanding foundation for the music educator. The professional areas of teacher training and additional linked pages that are timely, informative and interesting for anyone interested in music and education. The site has a wealth of creative and appealing technological advances that will certainly add to the teacher's repertoire. In closing, the main aim for one to study this site is to read the article written in September of 2004 by Tom Rudolph. Another very important reason is the wealth of information of technology and how it can aide in developing creative and interesting lessons that use technology. This is something the serious effectual music educator must consider.

Below are listed three very good sites that are excellent choices for educators to consider. They are recommended as resources that will add to the instrumental music teacher's toolbox. The review will be less extensive as the subsequent listed websites. The reviews will cover the following: title; web address; author's name; publication date (if listed); a short review; and a recommendation.

Title: *Educational Resources and Lesson Plans*
The user will locate below a quote found on the homepage. "This web page consists of thousands of links to lesson plans and other resources of potential use to current and future teachers. It also includes lesson plans and resources unique to this site. In most cases, I have provided brief descriptions of the content of the pages listed so that you'll know what to expect when you enter them."

Web Address:
*Educational Resources and Lesson Plans*
http://www.cloudnet.com/~edrbsass/edres.htm

*WebQuests Across the Curriculum*
http://cloudnet.com/~edrbass/webquest/html

Author: Edmund J. Sass, ED.D.
        Email: esass@csbsju.edu

Publication Date: Current

Short Review:
If the exploring educator scrolls down the homepage of this very prolific website, one will find *"WebQuests Across the Curriculum."* Click on that phrase and a wonderful page will appear. Listed are 350 WebQuests and resources. The page is divided into two large areas. The first area lists resources which contain links to: What is a WebQuest? WebQuest Locator; and Create a WebQuest. The second section is a listing of WebQuests by subject. There are several WebQuests listed in the music area. A few examples that seem very inviting are: *Searching for the Truth (African-American Music History); Brass Family Instruments; and The Jazz Era*. The teacher can explore several other projects and perhaps find a suitable WebQuest for the instrumental music classroom.

The site clearly suggests possible WebQuests to the teacher that are appropriate and doable for the age levels indicated for use. In addition, it is an easy task to locate projects within the site.

Recommendation:

The mother website *Educational Resources and Lesson Plans* is a substantial find for all kinds of enriching projects, lesson plans and teacher training. In addition, the WebQuest allows entrée to additional curriculum links which are great sources of information. This information puts the user in the point to find interesting and telling internet experiences for the teacher to discover and choose possible appropriate projects for the instrumental music student.

Title: *WebQuest News:*
   about the WebQuest Model, a constructive lesson format used widely
   around the world

Web Address: www.webquest.org/news/

Author: Dr. Bernie Dodge

Publication: A monthly news publication.

Short Review: This newsmagazine is published by one of the founding fathers of the WebQuest Dr. Bernie Dodge. Because of this fact, the publication is very relevant and current resource. Within the site, there are many articles that are salient and meaningful for the educator to read. As one reads these articles, additional suggested links are referenced. These links add to the overall article by giving excellent information that are very helpful to the teacher in garnering understanding as it applies to the WebQuest. In addition, located on the homepage is links to archival articles that are posted for the educator to research. The site also gives the professional the opportunity to read and post comments. This is a wonderful characteristic that allows for interactive actions that will certainly hold more interest, knowledge and sharing of pertinent information. Many comments are made by Dr. Dodge. It is a very inviting feature. Just think, one can interact with one of the originators of the WebQuest. The fact that one can comment and receive replies so quickly from the pioneer of the project is very attractive.

Recommendation:
WebQuest News is a premier resource for any educator in any field of study to have as a resource. Perhaps of the most important features of the website is the fact that it links to San Diego State University where the WebQuest was invented

and is the nation's leader in WebQuest activities. This link to SDSU ties directly to the university's WebQuest Database where there are many projects to choose from. All in all, the site is a wonderful, interactive and informational place to navigate.

Title: *Music 343: Teaching Music is the Middle School*

Web Address: http://www.camil.music.uiuc.edu/classes/343/multi_interdisc/webques_example

Author: Dr. Jason Meltzer and his students at De Paul University, Chicago, Il.

Short Review:
The website consist of a list 15 music WebQuests compiled by Dr. Meltzer and his students. These WebQuests are suitable for the middle school student. If one just clicks on to the web address that is on the homepage, the site will appear. The compilation of Webquests is an assortment of topics. The suggested sites contrast from country music to jazz to music history to music theory.

Recommendation:
This site is a fine for the instrumental music teacher to research potential projects or even give some ideas for possible future Webquests that the creative teacher might employ for his or her classroom. It is value looking into.

Below are listed two very high-quality sites that are excellent choices for educators to consider. They are music WebQuests that will insert to the instrumental music teacher's toolbox. As before with the resources reviews, each project will reviewed by the following criteria: Title; Author; Web Address; Publication Date; Short Review and Recommendation.

The next two music WebQuest reviews were found in the *WebQuest Across the Curriculum* website.

Title: *Searching for the Truth (African-American Music history)*

Web Address:

First one must go to the *WebQuests Across the Curriculum*

http://www.cloudnet.com/~edrbsass/Webquest.html

*Searching for the Truth (African-American Music history)*
http://www.manteno k12.il.us/webquest/high/Other/AfricanAmerican
MusicHistory/searchin.htm

<u>Author:</u> Created by Yvonne Walters (If the user wishes to contact
      Ms. Walters
      Email: <u>ywalters@olivet.edu</u>)

<u>Publication Date:</u> Not listed

<u>Short Review:</u>
The format of the home page is clear and very user-friendly for the student. All six of the parts of the WebQuest are listed with explanations that are clearly marked and appropriate for the high school student to use in an independent way. In addition, as the user opens the home page a musical melody is played. This creates additional interest in the project. Below is the opening comment made in the introduction section:

"African-American music is very universal, but it appears to be dying; the music industry needs your help. The President has commissioned The Museum Of Music and Art to create a display showing how African-American music has played a part in history, for Music History Month. The director of the museum is asking for your input."

This is a very engaging and inviting statement.

Following the introduction is:

- Task

- Process

- Resources

- Evaluation-Within this section, the creator has added an excellent rubric to guide the user in the completion of the project.

• Conclusion

Resources and credits follow. This area has some wonderful websites that link to critical information that assist in the accomplishment of the project. In addition, there is a link to a teacher's page.

Recommendation: The instrumental music instructor will find this project to an excellent well laid out project that will engage the student and give them a wonderful opportunity to learn about how African American music has given so much greatness to our American culture. It is attainable and is so well constructed that it will be a project that enhances the student's independent power because the student will have no problem navigating and completing the tasks.

The next music WebQuest found in the *WebQuest Across the Curriculum* website.

TITLE: *Music WebQuest (basic music theory and composition)*

Web Address:

First one must go to the WebQuests Across the Curriculum

http://www.cloudnet.com/~edrbsass/Webquest.html

Music WebQuest (basic music theory and composition)
http://www.nashua-plainfield.k12.ia.us/projects/chad/

AUTHOR: Chad Sowers

PUBLICATION DATE: Not listed

Short Review:

"Have you ever wanted to write your own piece of music but weren't exactly sure how to get started? Well now is your chance. With the help of a couple of excellent web sites, you are going to learn the basics of music theory and apply them by writing your own short composition."

Quoted above is found in the introduction of the homepage of this WebQuest. The objective is very clearly stated and inviting to the learner. Imagine a project that will give the learner tools that will aide in the creation of a personal musical composition. This is very stimulating stuff and allows the student to test, practice and develop a creative work of music. This will certainly test the students real understanding of the basic elements of music on a very personal level.

All six of the parts of a WebQuest are clearly cited with excellent explanations described. There are many supplementary helpful links that are provided to help in completing the mission. These links are very helpful and full of excellent appropriate and meaningful information that are essential to providing the proper tools to be successful in creating a short composition.

Recommendation:
The website offers an admirable project that is full of clear and doable activities. The process is well spelled out and will provide an excellent experience in Webquests and acquiring tools that will lead toward a successful creative activity. This Webquest is designed for the high school aged student and is so well done it will be not obstruct the student or get them bog down which leads to a dependent experience. This is what educators must judge when choosing a project. The question the educator must ask," Is it a doable exercise that will not lead to the teacher to continue to guide the student?" This activity is a very good project that will lead the student to a very nice experience that will result into independent power and a minimal amount of teacher intervention and direction.

Additional Music WebQuests Suggestions:

Below two music WebQuests are reviewed as possible internet projects:

Title: *Mozart Connection: Exploring the Power of Music*

This is another WebQuest that is found in the *WebQuest Across the Curriculum* website.

Web address:

First one must go to the *WebQuests Across the Curriculum*

http://www.cloudnet.com/~edrbsass/Webquest.html

Title: *Mozart Connection: Exploring the Power of Music*
*Mozart Connection*

http://projects.edtech.sandi.net/dailard/mozartconnect/index.htm

Author: Diane W. Pack

Publication Date: Not listed

Short Review:
This is a splendid project for the younger student. It is very appropriate for the elementary or middle school aged child. The homepage is very well designed with excellent graphics and very inviting and engaging for the learner. It has several links and suggested sites for the student and also the parent to review. All six parts of the WebQuest are clearly defined and spelled out for the learner. In addition, there are additional activities labeled as Fun Stuff to add to the interest of the experience.

The task which is quoted below tells it all. It goes beyond studying Mozart's music. It is a scientific exploration that investigates how classical music affects us.

Recommendation:
This is a wonderful well designed project for the younger student to experience the great music of one of the greatest composers. It is a must to consider as a meaningful internet experience. The project does aide the students in their quest toward musical literacy, historical understanding and how classical music affects us as human beings. It is a first-class blending of music and science which creates an appealing and exciting project.

The final review is:

Title: *Let's Make a Commercial*

Web Address: http://hceweb.rockdale.k12.ga.us/WebQuest_Proj/Music/Let.htm

Author: Jennifer Hurst

<u>Publication Date:</u> 2/18/2002

<u>Short Review:</u>

Task: The students create a commercial from its inception through the end of the complete production which involves writing, producing and performing.
The assignment as quoted directly from the homepage tells it all. It is a very interesting and engaging activity that will definitely create some real excitement for the middle age student. It is not only appropriate for the instrumental music student, but it can also be used by the general classroom experience.

All parts of the WebQuest are explained and very doable. In addition several links are suggested to help in accomplishing the project and an excellent rubric is provided to guide the students.

Another benefit for this project is that it concludes with a performance of each group. An excellent venue for the middle aged learner who really enjoy performances. Great for the self-esteem, poise and *e sprite de core* with a group activity.

<u>Recommendation:</u>
This is a well designed and fun activity to consider. The directions, resource links and tasks are clearly defined. The two valuable areas that one should deem is the fact that not only is the learner involved in a cooperative group community, but it also gives them a creative experience. This project works in two very important learning models-The Self-Expressive learning model which stresses creativity and the Interpersonal learning model which emphasis cooperative group learning. Both of these models are essential in our global workplace environments. This is a real winner for the instrumental music student or the general classroom situation. Wow! Where can the teacher provide an experience in which students create, produce and cooperate with each other?

The WebQuest allows the student the chance to raise their thinking skills in experiences of analysis, synthesis and evaluation. In addition, the WebQuest experience entails to take information and alter into useful and new meaningful knowledge.

# 5

## *Internet inquiry*

What is an Internet Inquiry?

The Internet Inquiry is an instructional model for students to find the answers to a question of high interest to them. The student delves into the question by developing independent research skills that provide opportunities to analyze synthesize and evaluate material.

Five Phases of the Internet Inquiry:

1.  Question Phase-During this phase the learner develops a specific or general question to explore. The teacher's role is to aid the student in his/her quest by:

    •  Assigning questions.

    •  Allows the student to select a question from a list.

    •  Provide a topic area that the student can create a question.

    •  Give the student the opportunity to construct a personal and meaningful question of their own.

2.  Search phase-Students can use the following strategies to investigate their selected question:

    •  Start the process with directories.

    •  Use search engines that prescreen material.

    •  Have the students share search strategies with each other.

3.  Analyze Phase-How can the learner analyze the information that is found during the search phase?

- Ask questions about the site.

- Look at the end of the URL (Uniform Resource Locator—the address of any Web document).

- Review each link.

- Investigate the relevancy of the site. How current is the information? When the site was last updated?

- Check and verify references.

4. Compose Phase-How will the information that was found through the Search Phase be assembled for presentation.
   There are three formats the learner can use to make the presentation:

   - Power Point

   - Written report

   - Video

5. Share Phase-There are three examples cited below that students can employ to share the findings of their investigation of their question:

   - Post their work on a classroom webpage.

   - Present an oral report.

   - Produce a multimedia slideshow.

<u>Reviewing Internet Inquiry Websites:</u>

The previous Internet project models had many wonderful examples and websites devoted to the respective model. Unfortunately, this is not the case in regards to the Internet Inquiry. The reason for this lies in the fact that the most important element of the Internet Inquiry is based on a question of great interest to the student. This is a personal task for the student and because of this there are too many variables to consider. The consequence is that there are not many examples of this model on the web. What was found is a number of sites that promoted the Internet Inquiry as a great tool to develop pertinent and meaningful skills for students to research, analyze synthesize and evaluate material. Below are listed some evocative sites to help the educator become familiar with the model and its benefits to the student:

*TeacherVision*

<u>Web Address:</u> http://www.teachervision.fen.com/internet/educational-technology/4514.html

This is a superlative periodical internet resource. If the instructor opts for a membership in this publication, they may sign-up for a free trial before subscribing. It is chalk full of many articles, lesson plans and other suggestive curricular material. The reason for including this issue in this chapter is the excellent article written by one of the most influential experts in the Internet Inquiry model Dr. Donald J. Leu. Dr. Leu has written a fine summary of the phases of the Internet Inquiry in an article entitled "About Internet Inquiry." This is a well completed piece that clarifies how the Internet Inquiry works and its importance as a tool for learning.

Dr. Leu's article http://www.teachervision.fen.com/internet/educational-technology/4514.html

He puts the model in view with the following closing comment that he makes in the article: "Internet Inquiry is a perfect vehicle for helping your students think critically and carefully. Students have so many questions about the world around them and there are so many resources on the Internet to engage them."

*Using the Internet to Promote Inquiry-based Learning* an epaper about a structured approach for effective student Web research.

<u>Web Address:</u> http://www.biopoint.com/inquiry/ibr.html

By David S. Jakes

   Mark E. Pennington

   Howard A. Knodle

www.biopoint.com

This is an excellent reserve for the educator. A must read and well worth ones time to surf through the website.

# 6

# _Teacher Resources_

This chapter is devoted to chronicling and reviewing a sample number of teacher resource websites. There are many teacher resource sites available on the World Wide Web, but just a few well known and popular sites are reviewed in this chapter. The main idea is to introduce these sites and perhaps spur the researching educator to find additional sites. As one explores these sites, perhaps others will be suggested within these sites. It just sort of snowballs as one navigates the suggested sites, others will be linked and may be more salient to the educators particular whims, interest and needs.

As in the previous chapters, each site will be reviewed with the following criteria:

- Title

- Web Address

- Author

- Publication Date

- Features

- Ease of Finding Information

- Current/Relevancy

- Amount of Information

- Recommendation

There are five sites that are reviewed. They are all premier sites that are general teacher resources that will help any educator. The user should locate these internet references and take some time to navigate and browse the site. There may be some information that would help and then again there may be some that is not relevant to the educator's particular classroom circumstances. The principal reason that the user should study these sites is awareness. Every earnest educator should have at there disposal a core teacher resource arsenal to draw knowledge from.

Below are the reviews of the following suggested core teacher resource sites:

- *Discoveryschool.com*
  Kathy Schrock's Guide for Educators

- *IPL Kidspace*

- *Teacher-to-Teacher Collaboration*

- *TeacherVision*

- *VirtualSalt*

(Please take note that the reviews of the websites that follow are introduced by alphabetical order and should not be construed as an order of the best down word. All of these websites are considered as exceptional sites that will enhance the educators, acumen, knowledge, and awareness, understanding and professional development.)

Title: *Discoveryschool.com*
          Kathy Schrock's Guide for Educators

Web address:
http://school.discovery.com/schrockguide/index.html

Author: Kathy Schrock

Publication Date: This site is continually up-dated "to include the best sites teaching and learning" as quoted from the sites homepage.

Features: "Kathy Schrock's Guide for Educators is a categorized list of sites useful for enhancing curriculum and professional growth. It is updated often to include the best sites for teaching and learning."

This is a quote also found on the website's homepage and it pretty much summarizes the information found within the site.

It is a very extensive website that features many ways for the user to find great amounts of real applicable and functional information for the educational development of the learner. In addition to the internet features, the site features lesson plans, classroom activities and many associated articles for the general consumption of educational information.

As an example, below the user will find areas on the homepage that link to even more links:

- Subject Access

- Kathy's Picks

- Teacher Helpers

- Search Tools

- Schrock's Guide Stuff

There is also a section devoted to contacting Kathy. The user can interact with Kathy by email which is a great source for any educator to have available.

Other areas of interest that are high highlighted on the homepage are: (Located on the left side of the homepage.)

- Curriculum Center

- Teaching Tools

- Homework Helpers

- Lesson Plans (If the user would click onto the Lesson Plan link, one would find a Fine Arts link.)

- Favorites (This area features: Study Starters and Puzzlemakers-create puzzles online.)

## Ease of Finding Information:
It is a very easy task to plot a course and find what the user is looking to attain. The homepage is very visibly marked and is not cluttered with useless graphics that just get in the way of finding the appropriate area of concern or links. The homepage also has an Alphabetic Index, Site Map and Search area clearly appointed. These all can be found on the homepage in the center area which is identified as Kathy's Picks.

## Current/Relevancy:
As referenced earlier in this review, the site is continually updated and monitored for the best and most current information, trends, issues and articles available.

## Amount of Information:
The site has literally volumes of information and related material to help and guide the informed educator. It is absolutely one of the most abundant sites in the education world today. It is manned by a person who has an impeccable reputation for excellence and meaningful information.

## Recommendation:

This site should be in all educators resource list. It is a priceless resource not only for its varied topics of information, but also for its validity and reliability. The educator will be amazed at the sites scope and merit in all areas of the educational realm.

Title: *IPL Kidspace (KidSpace@Internet PublicLibrary.com)*

Web address:
*IPL KidSpace*
http://www.ipl.org/kidspace/browse/tcn0000

*Internet Public Library*
http://www.ipl.org/

Author: The website is put together by a consorsium of colleges. The reader can check out the history of the authorship by choosing the About Us link located on the homepage.

<u>Publication Date:</u> This website is a continuing resource that is frequently updated in regards to information and additional material for the user to observe and research.

<u>Features:</u>
The user will find many sub-headings on the homepage. These sub-headings are diverse and very evocative in regards to the educational process. One of the sub-headings that are a particular interest to the instrumental music teacher is *Art Music and Museum Resources for the Parent and Teacher.*

Students are able to have an interactive experience by using the Ask the Librarian. By typing in a dialogue box, students 13 years old or younger can submit a question to the librarian. This is a very nice feature that is not only instructive, but also is fun for the student.

<u>Ease of Finding Information:</u>
This site is a real breeze in regards to getting from one place to another and navigating inside the site. Links lead to other links that refine a search even with more detail. The homepage is loaded with many phrases that lead to many links which in turn moves the user to even more links that are each more specific. This gives the user even more detailed information that leads to very comprehensive and inclusive study of the subject.

<u>Relevancy/Current:</u>
*IPL Kidspace,* as indicated above, this website is in continues change and updating. It consists of linkage that connects to very important and meaningful educational informational sites that is on the cutting edge of content and interesting topics that will augment the classroom activities.

<u>Amount of Information:</u>
As mentioned above, the site is prolific in each reach of information and coverage of the various sub-headings. Links move the user to additional links and detail that creates an environment of narrowing down major areas or topics to more specific information. The user can navigate as far as one wished to get a true picture of a particular subject.

Recommendation:
This is a very important website for educator to research. The best advice that one can give a user is to get on the site and investigate as far and as thinking "outside the box" as one desires.
Title: *Teacher-to-Teacher Collaboration*

Web Address:
http://teachnet.edb.utexas.edu/~Lynda_Abbott/teacher2teacher.html

Author: Lynda Abbott, Ph. D.

PUBLICATION DATE: This site is updated periodically. As of this writing, the last update was May 2007.

Features: This site is a "virtual" professional development exchange between teachers. A Teacher-to-Teacher website devoted to giving mounds of information and sources to teachers. The site is loaded with articles, sources and support information for the teacher. In addition, there is the opportunity to exchange and share with other professional educators.

Below are some of the areas of the content on the site:

1.  Teacher-to-Teacher Collaboration Sites

2.  Selected Teacher-to-Teacher and Resources Sites

    a.  Resources Shared by Teachers for Teachers

    b.  How-to and Other Information About Teachers

    c.  Discussion of Teachers' Roles in Professional Collaboration

    d.  Organizations Supporting Teacher Collaboration

By selecting the content areas and sub-areas, the user will find innumerable links.

Ease of Finding Information:
Just point onto the desired area or sub-area and the site easily moves to a number of very worthwhile and meaningful sites. It is a site that is clear, user-friendly and useful to any educator.

Relevancy/Current:
Dr. Abbott is frequently updating the website to make it a very up-to-date experience for educators. The site also has areas that are certainly beneficial for the student to surf through. It has so much information that it would be of value for anyone.

Amount of Information:
It is staggering the amount and meaningful information that is found in this site. The exchanging of information from teacher to teacher is in itself a fantastic opportunity for all to grow and share. Why re-invent the wheel. Share and all benefit.

Recommendation:
One marvels at the prospect the user will encounter while exploring and researching through this site. It is another example of a premier site that all educators must have in the arsenal of tools to assist and enhance learning in all educational pursuits. It is not only a superb site for curricular activities for the internet, but it is also a resource that will profit all areas of the educational process especially in regards to professional development.

Title: *TeacherVision*

Web address:
http://www.teachervision.fen.com/internet/educational-technology/4514.html

Author: Family Education Network's Teacher Channel

Publication Date: Current

Features:
Below is an article that is posted on the website. It is found by going to the homepage and clicking to the "About Teacher Vision" link at the bottom of the page.

"Family Education Network's Teacher Channel—TeacherVision.com
TeacherVision is the Internet's most popular teacher site for trusted online tools and resources that save time and make learning fun. Resources include a variety of lesson plans, free email newsletters and literature tie-ins, quizzes, and printa-

bles to help teachers easily enhance learning and incorporate technology into their classrooms."
This site is a current ongoing internet publication that is a paid site. It is a site that has many professional articles, lesson plans and printables for the classroom.

(Earlier it was recommended not to engage in paid sites. Sometimes there are worthwhile sites that afford great resources to the educator. It is valuable to look at this site and others that require a fee. The teacher is the only person to make the choice and it is a professional decision that should be considered. In the final analysis, the judgment should be based on personal preferences and budgetary deliberation).

Some related links that are located on the page that Dr. Leu's article as discussed in the review of the site in chapter five is displayed are:

- Internet Guide

- Communities with Online Groups

- Keypals

- Netiquette-Internet Etiquette

- Using the Internet for Teachers

At the very top of the homepage are the following tabs for additional pages:

- Home

- Grades

- Subject

- Lesson Plans

- Class Management

- Newsletter

- New Content

Each one of these pages is chock-full of additional links that really adjoin to the large amount of informative and meaningful material.

Ease of Finding Information:
This is a very user-friendly site that is clearly laid out with a well designed home-page. The user can navigate with ease throughout the site. This is a real positive aspect of importance that the user will certainly welcome.

Relevancy/Current:
TeacherVision is an online subscription website with current articles and resources. Resources that cover a myriad of topics and practical lessons, strategies and ideas that is continually updated and added.

Amount of Information:
Whoa! This a very comprehensive website that is loaded with educational information for all areas of the educational process. It has information which will lend a hand to the educator with internet curriculum matters and other general educational suggestions that will serve the educator in all facets of the educational process. The website has over 12,000 sources including downloads, printable lessons and other applicable and current educational articles and related information all designed to give the educator additional options, ideas and suggestions. The user can sign-up for a seven day trial to access the site. After the free trial, the annual fee is $29.95. The best suggestion is to take the seven day trial and navigate throughout the especially inviting site. You will be impressed with the amount and valid information that will be found.

Recommendation:
TeacherVision is one of the finest directories found on the internet. The user will be wowed by the amount of practical and significant information. It will make the educator always in the know of current educational findings and research that will be of great value for the classroom of today.

Title: *VirtualSalt*

Web Address: http://www.virtualsalt.com/index.htm

Author:
Dr. Robert Harris "taught at the college and university level for more than 25 years before retiring to write full time. He has written on the use of computers and software in language and literature study, using the Web as a research tool, the prevention of plagiarism, creative problem solving, and rhetoric. His most recent work centers on the integration of faith and learning. Dr. Harris holds the Ph.D. in English from the University of California at Riverside." (This is quoted from the website.)

Publication Date: July 2002

Features:
It is recommended constructively that the study of this site is an absolute necessity for any educator who is assigning research activities to his/hers students. It covers a wealth of information in regards to many areas of concern when students are researching information.

The homepage displays many worthwhile related links that will advance both the teacher and students quest in research on the internet and beyond. Below are several sections and each having links:

- Articles Related to Literature-Some of the links that are in this section are:
  - World Wide Web Research Tools
  - Evaluating Internet Research Source
- Articles for Students
- Articles for Educators
- Tools for Writers
- Tools for the Age of Knowledge
- Fiction
- Etext

Ease of Finding Information:
Finding the information and surfing throughout the site is very user-friendly. By simply pointing and clicking on the phrases, a large quantity of multi-topic information is available.

Relevancy/Current:
Some of the information is within 10 years or more, but the information is not outdated and germane. This information is always going to be current and used as standards in our present procedures. An example of this is located in the *Articles Related to Literature* one of the links is *A Handbook of Rhetorical Devises*. Within that link, there are definitions of over 60 traditional devises that students can use to improve their writing and reporting of the research they have found.

Amount of Information:
The best advice to the educator is to take a tour around the site and discover the appropriate information for all concerned. The information that is found in the site is staggering, appropriate and meaningful for all.

Recommendation:
The several sections and their related links are designed to provide generic and general information that will give students and educators many tools and information to aid the in enhancing the internet research activity experience.
This is a premier site for the educator to surf through. The idea that one has the website available will be very worthwhile. It is a tremendous resource to have and use when questions arise in regards to standards, definitions, tools and aids to assist both the educator and the student.

The educator can rest assured of the fact that is a first class website that is valid and a must to have for ones teaching arsenal of information that will ensure internet projects and general classroom success.

In closing, the reader should be aware of an outstanding website that is a collection of a large quantity of very useful and meaningful links to directories for all educators including the topic of music. It is worth the educator or student to take time investigating the websites assets within the site. It is another example of a superior resource. The title is: *Educators' Hot List*.

Web Address: http://www.ncsu.edu/ligon/teacher_resource.html

# 7

## _Music Resources_

Chapter seven exams three music resource websites in-dept and also introduces two websites as suggestions for possible music projects. The resource sites are extensive and give the educator many places to investigate and use for research. The suggested sites are introduced to the educator to give projects that are appropriate meaningful experiences. They are also given to generate potential ideas for the teacher to craft tailor made projects for use in the classroom. Later in the chapter, several websites will be recommended for the educator's toolbox as instrumental music research and information sources. These sites can be used by the instrumental music teacher as sites to give to the student for completing internet projects.

In-Dept Review of Resource Websites

Review Criteria:

- Title

- Web Address

- Author

- Publication Date

- Features

- Ease of Finding Information

- Current/Relevancy

- Amount of Information

- Recommendation

<u>Title:</u> *The Educator's Reference Desk\**
\*This site is an excellent all purpose resource that could also be listed in chapter 6 as a Teacher Resource. It is located in this chapter for the music educator to find music projects for the instrumental music classroom.

<u>Website Address:</u>
http://www.eduref.org/cgi-bin/print.cgi/Resources/Educational_Technology/
Computers/Internet/Internet_Projects.html

<u>Author:</u> The website is sponsored by The Information Institute of Syracuse.

<u>Publication Date:</u> Current

<u>Features:</u> The quote below is taken from the website and succinctly gives a summary of what this website is all about. As one can see, it is all encompassing in regards to valuable and useful information and ideas for the educator.

The Educator's Reference Desk provides access to:

<u>Resource Collection</u>—Links to over 3000 resources.

<u>Lesson Plans</u>—The Lesson Plan Collection of 2000 lesson plans.

<u>Question Archive</u>—A collection of over 200 answers of questions posed by other educators.

The homepage is clear and very easy to navigate through. At the very top of the page are four tabs. The four tabs are: Resource Guide; Lessons Plans; Question Archives; and Search GEM/ERIC.

(GEM is Gateway to Educational Materials of in access of 40,000 resources found on sites from local, state, federal and university Internet sites).

(ERIC is a search engine that is the most popular and quick resource for innumerable volumes of educational documents and information. It is supported by the United States Department of Education).

Educator's Reference Desk users may wish to search ERIC* at the U.S. Department of Education's ERIC website:

www.eric.ed.gov

*The Educators Reference Desk is not affiliated with or funded by the ERIC program or the United States Department of Education. All questions concerning ERIC should be addressed directly to the ERIC program at 1-800-LET-ERIC"

The second section found on the opening page is devoted to the following sections:

Home/Educational Technology/Computers/Internet.

The third area takes the user to two areas that have listed several sites to study. The two areas are: Internet Sites and Online Communities. The latter is dedicated to professional chat rooms and communication. An example site in this area is: Project Switchboard Chatboard. (Quoted from the site) "a project development and teacher networking center for teachers around the globe. Join our on-going discussion with teachers around the world developing Internet and inter-cultural projects."

http://teachers.net/projects/switchboard/

The former is a collection of several resource sites. Here is a sample site listed: Electronic Collaboration: A Practical Guide for Educators. (Quoted from the site) "This publication features an 11-step process for making online collaborative projects successful. The new guide also offers: explanations of various kinds of online collaborations—discussion groups, data collection & organization, document sharing, synchronous communication, & online workshops & courses; tools & websites that can be resources for creating each of these forms of collaborative environments; tips for moderating online collaborations."
http://www.alliance.brown.edu/pubs/collab/elec-collab.pdf

The last salient section to mention is located at the bottom of the homepage. The tab to explorer for the music teacher is Topics A-Z. By clicking on the tab, the user will find an extensive list of topics displayed. The user can find excellent resources for music. One will find a homepage for music that has listed horizontally the following sections: EduRef Lesson Plans; Archived Responses; Online Communities and Organizations. Under each of these quarters are a number of sites that can be very informative and useful to the music educator to explorer and use in the classroom.

Ease of Finding Information: This site is a breeze for the user to traverse thru. The links are organized by topics and are in an easy format. The user is motivated to survey further from site to site. They are appropriately organized and provide a clear and concise progression from site to site and give ample examples to travel.

Current/Relevancy: The website offers recent and trusted links to suitable and meaningful information for the educator to scrutinize.

Amount of Information: The website offers numerous topics and links to a variety of information to think about and research. This site is a very important entity that will help educators in all disciplines and is worth premier status in regards to finding an all purpose educators resource.

Recommendation: Fantastic!!! This is a website that is a must for all educators. It gives the educator a foundation for understanding resources and the possibilities of real pertinent information. The site is paramount in the pursuit of excellent ideas and support for educators to explorer.

Title: *K-12 Resources for Music Educators*

Web Address: http://www.isd77.k12.mn.us/music/k-12music/

Author: Contact person: Cynthia Mazurkiewics Shirk

Publication Date: Since 1995 and it is a current publication. The sites last update was September, 2007, as of this writing.

Features: A retrieved from the homepage. "Valuable resources for music educators and students of all areas and educational levels. Regularly updated.
For over twelve years, the most visited and valued music education resource website available internationally."

The homepage offers five major sections to explorer. The five sections are:

- Band

- Choral

- Orchestra

- Classroom

- All Music Educators

Each section has many supplementary links. The Band section links are very diverse in subject matter. The section is rich with links to such organizations as: College Band Directors National Association (CBDNA), and individual instrument societies like the International Trumpet Guild and jazz education sites such as Jazz in America/Thelonius Monk Institute. The Thelonius Monk Institute mission is:

"The mission of The Thelonius Monk Institute of Jazz is to offer public school-based jazz education programs for young people around the world, helping students develop imaginative thinking, creativity, curiosity, a positive self image, and a respect for their own and others' cultural heritage."

As one can envision from looking at the sample sites that are linked, they include a wealth of information for the educator or the student to survey in regards to research and meaningful and credible sources.

There are also other very important sections that are found on the homepage and like the previously discussed main five sections are also loaded with many valuable links. Additional sections are:

- Commercial Music Resources

- Music Research Resources

- Biographies, History and Works of the Great Composers

- Search Engines (ie: Google/Yahoo,etc.)

- Midi and Music Technology Resources

- Music Newsgroups

- Still More Music Links!

Each of these sections has many magnificent links that add to the prolific amount of information and evocative information for all to learn from.

Ease of Finding Information: As discussed above, the homepage is sizeable in range in regards to the various topics. The user only has to click on the appropriate link and it rapidly brings up the site requested. Also within each of these sites there may be additional links that are recommended. This is a very user-friendly site that is well formatted and trouble-free to use for the user's pleasure and advantage.

Current/Relevancy: The website is up-dated periodically with new resources and information. In addition there are many linked sites that are constantly up-dated with fresh information. Some of the linked sites are true tested and continue to be valid and relevant to the subject of music.

Amount of Information: The amount of information and topic areas are many. The linked informational sites suggest even further links and places to go for additional information. It is a snowball effect that gives the user many alternatives and suggestions for lessons and research that will aid the teacher and student in exploring and investigating music, instrumental music and many other related areas.

Recommendation: *The K-12 Resources for Music Educators* website is a premier resource directory. It is comprehensive in regards to the linked material that covers an array of music educational information and suggested lessons, activities and other useful significant information that will enhance learning for the teacher and the student.

> Title: *Music and Arts Library*
> (This site is part of the Columbia University Library Website)
>
> Web Address: http://www.columbia.edu/cu/lweb/indiv/music/offsite.html
>
> Author: The Columbia University Library Staff
>
> Publication Date: A current ongoing and up-dated publication.

Features: At the top of the homepage is what the website is all about. It lists the areas the site covers.

Selected Internet Resources in Music & the Arts

General Music Resources
Composition Ejournals Ethnomusicology Historical Musicology
Music Education Music Theory Online Audio Popular Music and Jazz Internet Search Tools"

As one can see, a very wide-ranging list of topics is available for students and teachers are able to investigate. The user can access many links that are listed under each of the topic areas.

"Red Hot & Cool Jazz—Large collection of links, including discographies and soundfiles." This is an example of one of the links under Popular Music and Jazz. In addition, next to the link there is a very helpful description of the content of the link. This is a very helpful feature that will save the user time in locating the appropriate information.

Another superb feature of the website is "Ask Us." This element allows the user to interact with the site. Some of the proceedings that the user can activate when using this feature is: ask a question; email a question; online chat service and other possible interactive dealings.

Ease of Finding Information: The ease at which the user can navigate through the website is indeed friendly and clear in its usage. The assortment of topic areas is clearly marked and the links that are parallel are identified and described to the content of the information found in the link. These linked sites are also first-rate in regards to their scope of information refectories and directing the user to additional related links.

Current/Relevancy: Because this website is a part of a major universities library system, it is evident that the information and its links that are coupled are compelling and meaningful sites that add to the body of consequential and worthy information.

The Ask Us feature of the website puts the educator or student in the position to interact with library staff members and experts in the field of study. This is an exceptional feature that ensures up-to-date information from a major learning institution.

Amount of Information: This site encompasses a large quantity of information. The main topics and their accompanying links are useful and authenticate.

Recommendation: As the other websites that are music resources that have been reviewed, this site is equivalent. It is an outstanding resource that will give support to all that use it. It is a professional instrument that is a premier index that will enhance the student and teachers repertoire of investigation tools.

Short Reviews of Music Resources
(Suggested Sites for Music
Educators and Students to Consider)

Review Criteria

Title:

Web Address:

Author:

Publication Date:

Short Review:

Recommendation:

Title: *Children's Music Workshop* (Music Education Online)

Web Address:   http://www.childrensmusicworkshop.com/instruments/flute/index.html

Author: Not named

Publication Date: 2007

Short Review: This website is sponsored by a commercial company that specializes in many areas of music education. The homepage has many excellent links that connect the user to such areas as: Music Resources; Instruments Music Links; and Advocacy. The site index is far-reaching and gives a variety of topics to explorer.

Recommendation: *The Children's Workshop* is a very informative tool for educators and students to navigate through. It is especially a great resource for the study of instruments. It is recommended very highly as a superb site to harvest useful information for research and information that can be used to increase understanding in regards to instrumental music and other music topics.

Title: *Music in the Yahoo Directory*

Web Address: http://dir.yahoo.com/Entertainment/music/Education

Author: Yahoo

Publication Date: Current

Short Review: This is a superb catalog that is so easily accessed. Yahoo is one of the most popular search engines. Many people are familiar with its value and ease of search process. The site is broken into three areas. The Categories section has many fine links. Some links found in this section are: Instruments; Festivals; Jazz; K-12 Curriculum Standards; Organizations and Web Directories. The second section is labeled Site Listings. Two examples of the links found in this section are: Royal Academy of Music and Woodwind Fingering Guide. The last section is Sponsors Results (commercial companies or private sector institutions). The Music Production Schools and Learn Music Production are examples of this sections links.

Recommendation: Another site that is an outstanding tool to have at ones disposal. Its ease of usage and familiarity too many is a real plus. In Addition, a prolific amount of information that will aid the investigation and exploration of many varied musical topics is a real value for the educator and the students.

Websites Recommended to the Educator as Good Sources of Information for Research and Information.
(These websites are ideal for students to use in completing internet projects)

Review Criteria:
Title:

Web Address:

Brief Description of the Website:

Title: *Classical Music*

Web address: http://42explore.com/classmus.htm

A Brief Description of the Website:
This website is a collection of many links that take the user to excellent amounts of information for researching. The site's areas of concern are composers and music history and literature. The site contains a wealth of meaningful useful information.

Title: *Classroom Internet Library*
       (Music Lesson Plans and WebQuests)

Web address: http://www.nhptv.org/Kn/vs/musla2.htm

A Brief Description of the Website:
This fine website consists of Lesson Plans; Ideas/Activities; and WebQuests. Each section as cited above links to numerous sites that are filled with excellent and interesting information that will certainly be helpful to the educator in designing projects for the classroom internet experience.

Title: *Internet Resources for Music Education*

Web address: http://www.cmeabaysection.org/resources.html#history

A Brief Description of the Website:

These spot is loaded with links to a variety of music topics. The topics include: Resources; Research; Technology; Theory; Conductors; The Families of Instruments (each having their own section); History and Literature; and Internet Links. In addition, there is an Alphabet Index of topics that make it very convenient for the user to investigate quickly. This site is a prolific directory that is worth an examination by the user.

Title: *Music 343* (Teaching Music in the Middle School)

Web address: http://www-camil.music.uiuc.edu/classes/343/multi_interdisc/ webquest_examples.html

A Brief Description of the Website:
A compilation of music WebQuest examples dedicated to the middle school aged student. The site encompasses a wide variety of music Webquests that will appeal to the assorted interests of the middle school aged student. An extremely advantageous directory that is an essential resource for this aged student. In addition, the site will act as an idea initiator for the educator to gather additional ideas for creating internet experiences that will augment the middle school instrumental musician's education.

Title: *The Internet Public Library*

Web address: http://www.ipl.org/div/subject/browse/hum20.60.00/

A Brief Description of the Website:
A leading informational site for the music educator to find suitable internet projects for the music student. A wonderful feature that this site has is the ability to ask a librarian for assistance. This site also links to several select sites that add additional related links to the mix.

Title: *The Physics of Musical Instruments*

Web address: http://www.glenbrook.k12.il.us/gbssci/phys/projects/yep/music/ muinet.html

A Brief Description of the Website:
This directory is dedicated to the study of the way instruments work. It is a scientific resource that the user can explorer the mechanical aspects of instruments and the production of sound through the study of acoustics. The site is full of excellent information links that puts the user in the how sound is made and other pertinent facts of science in regards to the study of the families of instruments. This is a valuable aid to the mechanically minded student or educator. There are a small number of suggested links found within the site that are no longer in operation, but the majority of the sites are operational and full of great information.

# Epilogue

The Epilogue is made of three sections. Section I will address the learning models, learning spaces and the internet models. I will show how these three learning entities relate to each other creating an awareness that will assist the teacher in providing adequate and positive projects that will help the student realize worthwhile learning goals.

The second area concerns the integration of internet projects into the instrumental music classroom. I will give some suggestions that might work for you. I am offering ideas that are designed to foster teacher creativity that will generate further thought for the teacher to investigate options for their classroom situation.

The final section is a summation of the major premise of this writing. The whole idea that is chronicled in this section is to encourage the educator to think beyond the training of literate musicians, but also encourage the professional to offer activities that will provide learning that will be instrumental in developing "learn how to learn" and "independent power."

I. <u>The Four Learning Models and the Four Learning Spaces:</u>

There are four learning models and for each model there are two accompanying strategies. In my book *Bravo!* I uncovered these models quiet extensively. If the reader is interested in exploring these models, I recommend that all educators study these truly excellent teaching models and their accompanying strategies. Below is listed the four learning models and in parenthesis is the prominent function:

- Mastery (Information)

- Understanding (Conceptual)

- Self-Expressive (Personal)

- Interpersonal (Life)

Each one of these models coordinate with each of the four learning spaces as described in Dr. David Thornburg's book *Campfires of Cyberspace*. Dr. Thornburg expounds on the learning spaces where real learning takes place. The four spaces and their corresponding function are in parenthesis:

- Campfire (Informational)

- Watering Hole (Conversational-Learning from Others)

- Cave (Personal reflection and Conceptual)

- Life (Contextual Real Life application)

Each of these spaces is where certain types of learning takes place. Thornburg makes the point that in each of the four spaces must be in balance with the other three spaces. All spaces in equal portions of time are essential for real meaningful learning to take place.

Below is a quote from *Bravo!* I recount the relationship between the four learning models and the four learning spaces:

"All four learning models make use of the four learning spaces of the Campfire, the Watering Hole, the Cave and Life. I see another connection. I equate the Mastery Model to the Campfire Learning Environment. This is the place where information is paramount. The Understanding Learning Model is related to the conceptual space where students are analyzing and doing critical thinking activities and reasoning. My contention is that the Understanding Model is related to the Cave Space where the student reflects on the information, reflects on it and comes up with there own personal connections. I also have found that the Self-Expressive Model is related to the Cave Learning Space. Students must find creative ways to make personal connections. In addition, the Interpersonal Model in my analysis is not only creating conditions that are conclusive to working with others in real life situations, but this model creates a great deal of conversational opportunities that coincide with the Watering Hole Space." (Palazzola 61)

Further Connections:
As I reflect further, I am going to make some additional relationships. I have studied quite extensively the four learning models, the four learning spaces and the four internet models and have found connections between all three of them.

Below is a chart that shows the correlation between all of the models and functions:

| Learning Spaces | Learning Models | Internet Models | Function |
|---|---|---|---|
| Campfire | Mastery | Internet Workshop and WebQuest | Informational |
| Watering Hole | Understanding | Internet Workshop | Conversational |
| Cave | Self-Expressive | Internet Inquiry | Conceptual and Personal |
| Life | Interpersonal | Internet Project | Contextual |

A quote from *Bravo!* sums my findings appropriately:

"This is an analysis that I have made and I feel will help the teacher create lessons and experiences that will give students more activities that will enhance the students learning opportunities that emphasis areas that perhaps they need more practice in certain spaces. As I mentioned earlier, all four of these models reflect all four of the spaces otherwise their learning would be missing spaces that are essential to meaningful learning. The reason why I bring this idea of mine up is to help you give your students more experiences in certain spaces that some models give more emphasis to particular learning spaces environments." (Palazzola 61)

If we take the chart listed above, we can assign appropriate lessons and activities that will enhance and make learning meaningful and fun.

Conclusion: My conclusion is that since a good balance of the four learning spaces and using the appropriate learning model the educator will select the proper internet model to achieve the goals and needs of the students. The correct internet model will be chosen and all three entities will be addressed. This will result in the teacher assigning excellent well thought out projects that will create superb and evocative learning occurrences by using the internet. Awareness in regards to how all of these learning, space, internet models will lead to worthy projects that will enhance the music curriculum, student understanding and aid in the area of the "holistic learning components"-LHTL and IP."

## II. Integrating Internet Projects in the Instrumental Music Curriculum:

The question we must ask is how can we integrate internet projects into the instrumental music classroom?

That is a very challenging undertaking to accomplish in any instrumental music situation. I can introduce some suggestions to stimulate the teacher on to further their creative and innovative ideas to achieve this task. But the answer will eventually lie within the teachers own particular situation, age level of students, curriculum needs and time considerations. As an instrumental music teacher, you are certainly aware of the time constraints, pressure of performance and general grade learning abilities and performance levels of attainment of your students.

In this section, I am going to make some suggestions to you that, in my own experiences and understanding of the school community, will perhaps help you to fit in this contemporary and vital activity of internet music projects.

## Elementary School:

As I study the possibilities of introducing internet music projects into the elementary students activities, I must admit it is possibly the most lucrative of the three levels. The best circumstances I am aware of is to act as a consultant with the homeroom teacher. Many times, the homeroom teacher is looking for possible topics and ideas for lessons and projects. Perhaps there is a student who is interested in instrumental music, general music topics or visual and the other performance arts. This is where the instrumental music teacher with his or her vast knowledge and familiarity with the arts can really benefit the homeroom teacher by helping and suggesting projects that are associated with the expertise of your field. Believe me they will welcome your help and consulting. Also remember that with your awareness of the various internet projects such as the Internet Inquiry, teachers give students the option of picking their own topic of research. You can really be an asset to the student and the teacher by cooperating and aiding any who needs your expertise and knowledge. My advice is to offer your services to any of the school community of your school to enhance and facilitate in regards to internet activities.

Therefore; I offer this idea strongly of acting as a consultant to your colleagues and students. As you know, it virtually is impossible for you to address the internet activities in your classroom situation. You have a limited amount of student contact time plus you are so involved in developing new and exciting skills to the beginning instrumentalist it is virtually impossible to accomplish this charge in your classroom. By acting as a consultant, you kill two birds with one stone. You help your colleagues and you also help give your young students internet experiences. A win, win for all. Bravo!

<u>The Middle School and the High School:</u> (I am clumping these two levels together because they are very similar in regards to the environmental classroom make-up and performance objectives.)

The middle school and high school instrumental music classroom is, as you are aware, the most difficult environment to integrate internet projects in the classroom. Since the secondary rehearsals are performance orientated, it is too much to consider taking large chunks of practice time away. This is where time management and creative lesson planning takes the vanguard. In my opinion, the optimum time for such internet activities is after performances and in between certain times of the performance seasons. These times are often welcomed by the students. By giving a short break periodically offend leads to even more enthusiasm when the students and teacher resumes normal classroom activities. For example: Let's consider the fact that there are natural breaks created during the school year. After the football season in the high school level, it is a good idea to change gears from the football band mentality and playing styles to the concert season. It can be described as a "cool down" time. I suggest taking a week or so before going into the new concert season to investigate some internet activity. The logistics could be a real issue, but here is where the teacher's creative and innovative ability can kick in. With some real creative scheduling and aid from the librarian and or technology coordinator, some very interesting use of time can be fashioned. Another example can be used for both secondary levels.

There are always those times during rehearsal where certain sections need to work on technical problems or on isolating certain areas in the music that need attention for certain groupings of instruments. Those groupings that need special attention can be efficiently addressed during a more homogeneous arrangement rather than a full rehearsal. In the long run, isolating and working on these problem areas with the smaller sectional format will increase the full rehearsals effectiveness and keeping the student interest and motivation alive because the problem areas and technical troubles are fixed without the laborious isolations of small groups. Many times this leads to boredom by the other students that are not involved. It is so important to keep as many active and on task as possible in the rehearsal environment. Keep the energy and activity going as much as possible to ensure effective and efficient progress. Here is where again creative and innovative scheduling and cooperation with the other school personnel can help. Provide internet projects to the students and rotate the sections in and out of the rehearsal room.

The high school level in many schools offer advanced placement and independent study that allows students to explorer in an in-depth manner a particular subject area. Those students that choose this option have the opportunity to investigate and research subjects that interest them. What a wonderful chance to study beyond the regular classroom curriculum concerns. Much of this work is done on an individual basis with teacher guidance and facilitation. By using the various internet projects outlined in this writing is a great chance for the students to acquire understanding and new and useful information within the music area of study.

In the middle school level curriculum, it is found that many schools offer gifted education for the more advanced student. Here is another place where students can traverse the internet projects to learn and gain individual information as either a student of music or even those students not involved music, but who are very interested in advancing and enhancing their personal understanding of music. The music teacher acts a consultant to the gifted teacher. The gifted teacher will love your participation and expertise. All learn and all will win.

A Review of the Major Premise of the Book:
The Synopsis in summation describes that it is imperative that in this new century some heroic changes are inevitable in the educational process of America. These changes are slowly beginning to make their presence known in the educational institutions. Within the new landscape, it is evident that there is more and more emphasis on learning communities and cooperative learning models. The reason of this phenomenon advancing is the fact that these models are replicating the new global workplace environment. Our world is shrinking in regards to the marketplace. Workplace activities are dedicated more toward cooperative groups that actions are dedicated toward problem solving, creativity and innovation of new ideas or ways of doing business. Technology has changed advanced the total global environment. Many countries are able to be players in a world economy because of technology. In addition, many governments have made business

opportunities much more advantageous for its citizens and corporations by making positive trade policies that support their success.

Because of this contemporary global reality, the world is flat once more as it was considered in the 15^Th. Century. This fact is chronicled very well by Thomas Friedman in his book *"The World Is Flat."* I recommend this book highly to any educator. It is well written and researched. Mr. Friedman paints a very interesting picture of where our planet is progressing in regards to economic and also political relations. These facts that are brought to our attention in this book have great ramifications to our American educational system. Educators must be aware of these facts and adjust the curriculum to embrace the data and reality which is described. We must ensure that our students are prepared to take on the new challenges that face our country and guarantee we keep our place in the world and remain in a position of supremacy.

Advancing this point, I want to re-state a quote that is found in the Synopsis of this book. This quote embodies my major premise of this manuscript.

"American education must be in the lead in regards to keeping this country in the forefront of innovation and progress. It just makes sense that if would we want to remain as the leaders of the world a great effort must be given toward making sure we give our people the tools to succeed. I envision that today's educators have two areas to work on that will ensure that our young people will have tools to compete as all disciplines across the curriculum must have these two ingredients as components.

I will label each area as a holistic learning component. Each of these two (HLC) can be addressed by using the four learning models, multiple educational strategies, pedagogical, motivational and presentation techniques. These skills, strategies, models and techniques are the tools to accomplish the two holistic learning components that will produce the outcomes in our students that make them the best they can individually be and continue to raise our national standards and innovative creativeness that makes our people the world leaders in all areas.

The first holistic learning component (HLC) is "learn how to learn," (LHTL). All of our energy in the educational process must direct itself toward teaching students how to learn. In my opinion, the teacher's first responsibility is to give the student as many tools, experiences and practice in order to learn as an individual. The means to accomplish this LHTL will very from grade level, course or discipline. But the end is universal. Everything leads to LHTL. Putting in another way is: the means may be different, but the ends are to one goal. "Learn how to learn."

The second holistic learning component (HCL) is connected to the "learn how to learn" (LHTL). If a learner is able to "learn how to learn," they have "independent power" (IP). Further investigation into these two components and how they are connected, one can say you can't have one without the other. In order for one to be able to "learn how to learn," there must be a utilization of all of the knowledge, information, understanding, learning strategies and techniques one has available in the learners tool chest in order to solve complex problem or reach understanding.

Perhaps another way to describe the inter-relationship between the two learning components is to offer the following football metaphor:

The "learn how to learn" is the play (which results in a score) as "independent power" is the pass or run (which is the technique needed.)

Independent power is an on going process. It never stops. Individual learners are constantly discovering new ways to increase the number of learning tools to add to their tool chest. The more have the more power.

One of the teacher's prime responsibilities is to provide as many opportunities for students to be aware of as many strategies. This will enable the student to increase their individual power.

The purpose of this book is to bring to the attention of the instrumental music teacher IP tools to be used with the internet. Instrumental music teachers not only must continue to provide leadership in teaching students performance skills and interpretation of the written score, but assist in the total education of the individual student. In fact, all disciplines and courses must work across the curriculum to ensure that all students "learn how to learn" and obtain as much "individual power" as possible."

In closing, the instrumental music educators must remember their responsibilities to their students. It goes beyond the imparting and transferring of musical knowledge, giving aesthetic awareness experiences, teaching of instrumental music technical skills and giving performance opportunities. In my opinion, it is essential that instrumental music teachers go beyond the purveyors of music literacy of the written score as outlined in the previous sentence. Below is an equation that describes my mission that I believe is the essence of music education: (This equation goes beyond the one in Chapter I of this writing because it is a more complete picture of the total mission. The equation takes into account the music literacy component.)

TTWS+IT+LHTL=ML+OTBIAC
Or
Teaching the written score + Independent Power + Learn how to Learn = Music Literacy + Opportunity to be Innovative and Creative.

All of this results in the reality that instrumental music educators should be aware that the tools of educating are expanded to accommodate the new mission that I have expressed. The educator of instrumental music is artistic, innovative, and creative. Since we possess these traits, we must expose these concepts to the students that we are entrusted. By using as many strategies and tools such as the internet in our presentations of our craft and art, we are enhancing the curriculum and experiences to the student that will allow them to be successful in the workplace, understanding the art of music and other meaningful endeavors that make them fine citizens and human beings. The activities of the internet will certainly energize and motivate students toward a better understanding and awareness of the discipline of music and the world and its complex environs. The internet is a vehicle that garners additional tools to promote the nurturing of skills and literacy's that support multiple learning experiences.

Thank you, (Please let me know your thoughts.)Joseph V. Palazzola
musicstrateiges@bellsouth.net

# References

Friedman., T. *The World Is Flat* : *a brief history of the twenty-first century* (2005). New York City, NY. Farrar, Straus and Giroux.

Jordan., E. *Integrating the Internet into the K-12 Curriculum* Study Guide. . Masters in the Art of Teaching. Marygrove College. (2004). Detroit, Michigan. Canter Educational Productions.

McClanaghan. *Models of Effective Teaching* Study Guide. Masters in the Art of Teaching. Marygrove College (2001). Detroit, Michigan. Canter Educational Productions.

Palazzola. J. *Bravo! Strategies for Music Educators* (2006). Lincoln, NE. iUniverse Publishing.

Thornburg., D. *Campfires in Cyberspace* (1996). San Carlos, CA. Starsong Publications.

# *About the Author*

**Joseph V. Palazzola** has been in the field of music education all of his adult life. Mr. Palazzola has taught in both public and private schools for 36 years. He has taught on the college level for seven years in the teacher training area. Presently, he is retired and resides in Vero Beach, Florida.

musicstrateiges@bellsouth.net

978-0-595-49314-2
0-595-49314-9